FOR JUDY

*Staunchest Ally*
*Closest Companion*
*Dearest Friend*

# Praise for *The I Ching for Writers*

"At last, an indispensable writing book that persuades us to gamble Eastern style, with an honorable sensibility. The stakes are high, for if we cast our lot with Sarah Jane Sloane and her *I Ching for Writers,* we're making a serious investment in our writerly selves. Sloane's path to the numinous requires three ordinary pennies, paper, pencil, and a reliance on things both mystical and practical, offered by a wise and courteous croupier who's on our side, gently coaxing us to take chances, to keep playing."

— Leslee Becker, author of *The Sincere Café* and professor of English at Colorado State University

"As a seeker who's consulted the I Ching's wisdom for many years, I'm thrilled to discover a new book of interpretations as seen through the prism of writing. Just the names of the hexagrams themselves promised an oracle that would speak directly to what matters most to me — my writing. I could hardly wait to throw my first hexagram. If you're a seeker like I am, or simply curious, I encourage you to let this wonderful oracle reveal its magic to you. Thanks, Sarah Jane Sloane, for creating this relevant, new translation of an ancient wisdom."

— Judy Reeves, author of *A Writer's Book of Days*

"Sarah Sloane's *The I Ching for Writers* is a rare find: a writing guide that is itself delightful to read. Dr. Sloane provides wise counsel here. Her advisories offer astute assessments of the writing process (and of life in general);

her exercises are unique and inventive but grounded in the practices of a skilled writing teacher. This book is rich and engaging. I look forward to using it with my students in my courses on creative nonfiction!"

— Cynthia Cox, director of writing programs and associate professor of English at Belmont University

"A sure cure for writer's block, this book is great for creative brainstorming and keeping works in progress progressing. A good addition to any writer's reference shelf."

— Hal Zina Bennett, author of *Write from the Heart* and *Writing Spiritual Books*

"Those who struggle with writing — and they are legion — know in their bones what it feels like to be wordless and silent. Into this uneasy space steps Sarah Jane Sloane, with a dazzling display of imaginative advice for writers in *The I Ching for Writers: Finding the Page Inside You.* Take this journey with Sloane as she works through what the I Ching's sixty-four hexagrams can tell you about your writing self; then see how your imagination takes up the writerly challenges offered here. Most of all, do as Sloane instructs: 'Find the connections, listen with the inner ear to the secrets of the heart.' You may well be surprised, and greatly heartened, by what you hear."

— Andrea A. Lunsford, professor of English and feminist studies, Stanford University

# THE I CHING
# FOR WRITERS

# THE I CHING
## FOR WRITERS

### FINDING THE
### PAGE INSIDE YOU

SARAH JANE SLOANE

NEW WORLD LIBRARY
NOVATO, CALIFORNIA

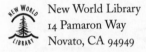

New World Library
14 Pamaron Way
Novato, CA 94949

Cover design by Mary Ann Casler
Interior design by Tona Pearce Myers

Library of Congress Cataloging-in-Publication Data
Sloane, Sarah.
   The I Ching for writers : finding the page inside you / Sarah Jane Sloane.
      p.   cm.
Includes bibliographical references and index.
ISBN 1-57731-496-4 (pbk. : alk. paper)
   1. Written communication. 2. Yi jing. I. Title.
P211.S62 2005
808'.02'01—dc22                                    2004023296

First printing, March 2005
ISBN 1-57731-496-4

Distributed to the trade by Publishers Group West

10  9  8  7  6  5  4  3  2  1

# CONTENTS

# ACKNOWLEDGMENTS

The people who help me most with my writing are those whose conversation and character give shape and meaning to my life.

I am particularly grateful to my mother, father, and brother for their support and love.

Rare teachers, people who genuinely nurture their students, for me include Andrea Lunsford, Beverly Moss, Cynthia Cox, Rich Enos, Anne Herrington, Marcia Curtis, Sara Stelzner, and Charlie Moran. More recently, Donna LeCourt, Lisa Langstraat, Mike Palmquist, Kate Kiefer, Sue Doe, and Liz Jackson have shown me what a dedicated and collaborative faculty can do.

Buddhist practitioners, members of the Gurdjieff community, longtime throwers of the I Ching, alternative health practitioners, or seekers in general who have helped me include Susan Aposhyan, Patrick Brennan, Susan Brown Carlton, Matt Cary, Monica Kaup Cary, Tammas Kelly, Brody LaRock, Carroll Smith, and Stuart Smithers.

I thank my agent, Sheree Bykofsky, and my editor at New World Library, Jason Gardner. Thanks to Carol Venolia for her gentle copyediting. And many thanks to Craig Hollow for our conversations and the photographs.

Finally, writer Judy Doenges — best friend, inimitable ally, and fierce protector — has helped me steadily in every way for the last twenty years. To her I dedicate this book.

# INTRODUCTION

## *The I Ching and the Trouble with Writing*

When you are up against the wall and can't think of a thing to write, frustration sets in. I tell my students it's like being in a vehicle with no gas, no tires, no map, and no road ahead. You can't get traction no matter how hard you try. And after a long day or night of trying to write, other responsibilities intervene: a meal must be cooked, the pets fed, your children put to bed, the newspaper skimmed, your partner's day heard, and still you have written nothing. At night you do anything you can to avoid the blank page, including watching TV or going to the movies. There's nothing inherently wrong with these activities, but they distract you from the hard work of putting words on a page, one after another, day after day. They keep you from discovering what it is *you* want to write — and from faithfully writing it down. At times like this, sometimes a suggestion from outside your own mind can prime the pump. I offer this adaptation of the I Ching to feed your imagination and get you writing for real.

## FEEDING YOUR IMAGINATION

Feeding your imagination is one of the most important activities of a writer, as the poet Madeleine DeFrees once told me. The imagination is something like a Southern "conjure-woman" or sorceress, who hides and spins spells deep into the night. Your feelings of intuition are simply her breath on the back of your neck. To keep the conjure-woman happy, you have to feed her with stories and music and just being wild.

And when you stand at a crossroad in the night with the conjure-woman at your side, she may start paying attention if you spin a tale or two. Or if you write from the heart and discover your own voice, then you may catch the conjure-woman watching you. And if you tell the truth, whole and brilliant and sad, you've caught her. She'll eat it up. The sharp wind of imagining will sweep across your mind and stir up the unexpected.

The conjure-woman shows us the value of playing, of juggling feelings and words until they find some deep resonance in our heart. Her appetite guides us to consider what feeds our lives and our writing. Are you a scattered thinker, someone who wonders about the stars' constellations one second and the traffic patterns in lower Manhattan the next? Use it. Do you work outward from a single observation, slowly building up the system that arises around it? In other words, do you stare at the air conditioner fixed to the window opposite, then let your mind wander toward the effects of increased electricity consumption in summer? Use it. Develop your imagination by granting it experiences that expand your palette. Study your own mind as it plays with those experiences. Play with the I Ching. Choose people and places that excite your writerly side. Visualize and write about them all.

Write everything down. Write and rewrite and rewrite some more.

Feed your imagination by reading, too. See how other writers have faced the blank page. Listen to the pages of a good writer working, study how she structures a scene or he develops a character, enjoy the sound of a sonnet, and be inspired. Think about the original meaning of *inspiration,* one that both T. S. Eliot and Geoffrey Chaucer certainly knew: to breathe in, to take in the fresh air of other writers, musicians, or artists. It can be marvelously bracing to watch other writers do their work.

And as the writer Dorothea Brande explained more than fifty years ago, another task of the writer is to choose friends and experiences that invigorate you, that get those creative fires burning. Choose writers' groups and friends that leave you wanting to write and revise, not those that leave you enervated and exhausted. Choose friends who recommend good books and energize you with their conversation. Avoid people who suck you dry, who are what a friend of mine calls "energy vampires." Feed your imagination constantly, and your writing life will be nourished too.

## COMING TO TERMS WITH YOUR FEARS

Or maybe fear is your worst demon. You are afraid that if you start to write it will never measure up. That you won't get it right the first time. That you have no idea what direction you're going in anyway, so why start? And if you start and it isn't any good, you've dashed your most important dream: the dream of having friends, even strangers, listen to what you wrote down. The wisdom of your true self will be obscured, even when what you have to say may be really, really important. Should you even try?

It is far easier to not even try. To not take risks when you do start. Or to never show anyone else what you have written when you write. The bad news, or the most interesting news, is that there is no way to write risk-free. So even when you are too frozen to begin — and who can blame you? — it's important to start taking small steps. The important thing is to face your fear head-on, acknowledge it, even welcome it as it comes and goes. Because fear fuels your imagination, too. Fear is that familiar presence at the back of your mind that needs to be invited in so you can get on with your writing. You need to invite fear into your living room so it can help you write with all of yourself present.

I once took a workshop from Tsultrim Allione, an inspiring Buddhist teacher who taught us how to cut through our fears of sickness, accidents, or death: visualize them as a person or creature who needs to be fed, then feed them all they want until they are glutted. So that's what I did, and it worked. And that's what I am recommending to you: defeat your fears by inviting them in out of the rain. Work with your fears rather than ignoring them, and you will write better. Talk to your fears, personify your fears, develop a relationship with them that is friendly rather than adversarial. Don't let fear freeze you, or make the engine seize up, or force the pencil to drop from your hand. If the day's I Ching prediction warns that you are in grave danger, slow down. But do not stop writing. See your fear as a close and unpredictable ally that can help you write your best. Open the door and invite it in for a cup of coffee. Meet danger, not with bravado but with steady courage. Embrace your fear; look it in the eye; write down everything it says.

Some of the I Ching hexagrams in this book will contain warnings; some will help you; and some will advise you to celebrate your writing, your life, your family, your friends. All these advisories are accurate at some point in the process. Put together, they are saying this: Be steady as a writer; celebrate your writing; and be courageous in your own brief life.

## WHY I WROTE THIS BOOK

I've been teaching writing to college students for over twenty years, and I have some ideas about what works. I know I can show you ways to feed your imagination and show you what some other writers say about the challenges of writing. I want to help you overcome your fears, to help you imagine new people and places. I want to encourage you to give your imagination a workout — and to get to know that part of your mind that visualizes the past, present, and future. I want to help you know your own mind, and the minds of other people, by putting little marks down on a page.

I want to write something that will inspire *your* writing.

I hope this book will be an intuitive map to help you find your way in composing stories, poems, plays, or creative nonfiction. I hope this book will give you a safe place to explore your own writing process. In short bursts. In a place where what you write isn't evaluated and the fact that you actually *are* writing is celebrated. I hope the book will energize you and inspire you to write true tales, fiction, poetry, plays, and whatever else you want to write.

I hope that this book will also teach you respect for the marvelous tool of Chinese divination, the I Ching. Somewhere between a playful exercise and an eerily accurate divination device, each I Ching hexagram reveals a truth, and dares you to become the writer that you already are. By throwing the coins and performing hexagram readings[1] in *The I Ching for Writers,* you will be able to jump-start your own writing process while reading a prediction of where your writing might go. Say you've gotten up an hour early this morning, poured yourself a cup of steaming hot coffee, and are ready to write. You might use this book to help you get started, to prime the pump. Or maybe you write for a living and

---

[1] As I will explain in greater detail later in this chapter, "throwing" the I Ching is a simple gesture of tossing three coins up in the air six times. Each toss defines a line in a "hexagram," which is your fortune for the day — e.g., revise, work on the ending, shorten your text. In this book, each hexagram is accompanied by some advice, a prediction, and writing exercises. See page 13 for more details about this process.

have hit a rough spot; throw the coins and do one of the exercises to limber up. Or you're a pretty good writer who is suddenly stymied by the wide blank page. You could turn to the extra exercise for hexagram 43 to get around your writer's block. No matter what the trouble, more often than not the writing exercises and games fostered by this adaptation of the I Ching will help you over the hurdle.

## A SHORT HISTORY OF THE I CHING

Five thousand years ago, a giant turtle crawled out of the Yellow River and revealed the secrets of writing and the I Ching at the same time. Both were symbol systems inscribed on the back of its huge carapace. The emperor Fu Xhi was the first to understand the significance of the black markings on the turtle's shell. He correctly saw them as symbols that stood for things (writing) and offered predictions (the I Ching). The two activities have been closely aligned ever since. And the mythic turtle that climbed out of that river became the basis of the ancient Chinese belief that a cosmic tortoise holds up the whole world. Metaphorically speaking, it isn't too absurd to say that writing holds up the world. The words you write, the phrases you string together, can become a work that changes your world or the world of others, permanently.

The sixty-four hexagrams that the turtle brought out of the river revealed the fortunes of royalty, ordinary people, and whole countries. These hexagrams offered advice about everything under the sun. The I Ching was able to give those who used it a fuller sense of themselves and their potential. Literally meaning "book of change" ("I" means *change*, and "Ching" means *classic* or *book*), the I Ching not only helps its users understand the future; it helps them understand their present circumstances and the distant past.

Fu Xhi took these two tools — writing and the I Ching — and taught them to the people in his kingdom. Within just a few months, diplomats and ministers everywhere in China were practicing the new arts of writing and divination. Taoists started applying hot pokers to pieces of turtle shell to divine the future. Called oracle bones, these pieces of shell split under the pressure of heat and the resulting lines would indicate a "yes" or a "no" to the diviners. However, the diviners soon realized that this binary system was too limiting, and oracle bones became a thing of the past. I Ching prognosticators began to toss yarrow stalks instead, producing hexagrams that described the future in far more subtle and insightful ways. Soon scholars and Taoists were writing commentaries about the I Ching, offering detailed interpretations of what it revealed.

Through the succeeding centuries, Fu Xhi's knowledge of writing and the I Ching passed to three important scholars: King Wen, the Duke of Chou, and Confucius. Confucius was especially fascinated by the I Ching, and he is reported to have broken the bamboo binding of his copy three times in his enthusiastic reading. Followers of Confucius took to reading the I Ching and its new commentaries, by then formally known as *The Book of Changes*, in small folded volumes known as "butterfly books." In the seventeenth century, a Christian missionary in China wrote to the German philosopher Leibnitz and told him about the I Ching. Leibnitz got curious about it and started exploring its possibilities. His interest spurred others in Europe to study it. Gradually, people began to use the I Ching not only for prediction, but for contemplation of their own place in the cosmos. Since that time, the I Ching has been used in the West as well as in the East.

The I Ching is still a marvelous tool for analyzing the self and our hidden motivations. Writers will find its prognoses especially useful.

## THE I CHING TODAY

When scholars stopped using oracle bones to predict the future, they turned instead to a complicated system that used bundles of yarrow stalks. Throwing the yarrow stalks on the ground over and over until the six lines of a hexagram were determined is the source of our expression today of "throwing" the I Ching. However, throwing yarrow stalks was soon replaced by a much simpler system: casting three coins. That system is the primary one used today.

Over the last four centuries, the commentaries and interpretations of the I Ching have grown vast. Today the I Ching is used not only for prognostication but also for understanding the mysteries of human nature. Some people throw the I Ching to understand conflicts in the contemporary workplace, and others to predict world events. Still others throw the I Ching to determine which way the stock market will swing or whether they should get a divorce. Some use it as a mirror to understand themselves and events happening in the present. Whatever issue is at hand, the I Ching can add a dimension to considering it. And no matter who asks the question, the I Ching can respond.

I don't know whether the I Ching accurately forecasts how things will be. But I do know that the skills we bring to interpreting it — the way it forces us to build a web of meaning out of its sixty-four scenarios — are necessary skills of the imagination. And feeding the imagination, coping with fear, and overcoming writer's block — short or sustained — are the things this book is designed to do.

## HOW THIS BOOK WORKS

The I Ching introduces the element of chance into your writing. It will surprise you with its accuracy and give you some new writing challenges to chew over. Every hexagram in this adaptation of the I Ching is directly related to the process of writing and becoming a writer. This book makes writing a little more fun, and it teaches you about a time-honored Eastern tradition while you develop as a writer. I'll show you how to ask a good question and throw the I Ching to get an answer. I don't want to say that the hexagram you discover is an absolutely accurate prediction of your future as a writer. But I do want to say that, in my experience of throwing the I Ching for more than twenty years, there have been some stunning coincidences between a hexagram and what happened next. For example, I got a new job as a professor just after the I Ching told me to expect change in my work life and to prepare for a conversation with a new and powerful person (the dean at my new university). You will read in the last chapter about what happened when I threw the I Ching in regard to this very book.

The commentaries I've written for these hexagrams will provide a new way for you to think about your life as a writer. From the I Ching, you will learn how to turn your dreams of writing something that people will care about into reality. This is a book designed to get you started on such a path — or, if you already have started, to keep you going.

## EUREKA! HEURISTICS FOR WRITERS

*Heuristics* is a Greek word that comes from the same root as *Eureka!* — a cry of discovery, a sense of finding the way. Heuristics for writers are invention exercises designed to prime the creative pump. The main point of this book is to give you some heuristics, to let you play more with language, to find a new way of creating the stories you want to tell. But you can play here in ways that don't have to lead to the Great American Novel. Maybe one of the exercises in this book *will* lead you to write something longer and better. Maybe it will get you on the road to writing something that other people must hear. But in the meantime, you have permission to make huge and grand mistakes. To write something that starts out captivating and then does a nosedive. Or the other way around. You'll limber up your muscles and find new ways to blend reality and fiction, or poetry and dream. And you'll find commentaries that bring your writing life into new relief.

By throwing the I Ching and following the guidelines in this book, you will get to compose yourself as a writer at the same time as you write. Yes, you will discover what you have to say. But also, through the intervention of chance and intuition, you will learn more about who you are. There is a glossary at the back of this book to help you with some of the more technical terms of writing poetry and fiction.

Ultimately, *The I Ching for Writers* is a way to gain perspective on who you are as a writer, and where your writing can take you.

Again, today's commentaries to the I Ching must be read as suggestive rather than definitive. There is no case in which the hexagram alone will reveal the future. You must apply your own common sense and reason to your readings. It can be both fun and serious to interpret individual hexagrams, and it is likely to get you excited about who you are as a person and as a writer. Nevertheless, it is important to remember that the accuracy of a hexagram's predictions depends on your expertise and the depth of your analytical skills.

## USING THIS BOOK

One way to use this book is to keep a notebook of the writing you do every day in response to a hexagram. Later you might find a great idea in that notebook, a springboard to some longer or fuller composition. Or you can use this book to stimulate discussion between you and another writer; the two of you might write together once a week, then share what you have written in response to your respective hexagrams. Finally, writers' groups have used this book to start a meeting by having all the members write to a single hexagram's suggestions and then reading aloud what they have written.

However you choose to use this book, I do recommend that you keep all your I Ching writings in one place. In that stack of completed exercises, you just might discover some patterns of image or theme — or, even better, a great idea for future writing.

It helps to have some work-in-progress at hand so that the I Ching can offer advice about something you are writing. If you aren't currently working on anything, before you consult the I Ching write a page or two about the first time you did something: rode a bicycle, kissed someone, got a paycheck, went to the ocean, smoked a cigarette. That exercise will give you some pages to which you can apply the I Ching's advice.

### HOW TO CONSULT THE I CHING

There are five steps to consulting the I Ching: framing the question, throwing the coins, scoring the coins, identifying the hexagram, and interpreting the hexagram. That sounds more complicated than it really is; after a few tries, this process will become second nature and you will be on your way to becoming an expert.

## *Framing the Question*

Good questions result in good answers. Framing the appropriate question is difficult and important work. First, think about the topic you want to explore. Then frame a question in such a way that it isn't going to yield a "yes" or "no" answer; such questions are simplistic, and they produce unreliable results when throwing the I Ching. In other words, don't ask, "Will I be a successful writer someday?" but ask instead, "What should I do next to make my current writing project successful?" "What" questions tend to work best. Choose a question that gets as close as possible to your heart's real core.

Some examples of good questions are:

- What activities are auspicious for me to undertake today?

- What is my biggest obstacle to becoming a writer?

- What's the next step in this project?

- What should I write about?

- What will be the outcome of this project?

- What do I need to do to write more?

Once you have framed the right question, write it down on a piece of paper in front of you. Say it aloud and make any revisions that will sharpen the question. Stare at it until you have memorized it and can see it in your head. Focus your entire attention on the question you have framed.

## *Throwing the Coins*

One of the easiest ways to "throw" the I Ching today is to use three ordinary pennies.

Get a piece of paper and a pen or pencil. Find a flat surface and clear away any clutter. Hold three pennies between your palms, concentrating on the question you wish to ask. Rub and roll the pennies between your palms, or in one hand. Ground yourself, feeling your feet take root through the floor. Think in a general way about yourself as a writer. See your question inside your head. Then throw the coins onto the flat surface.

Note how many heads and tails you have thrown and write them down. This will become the bottom line of the hexagram you are constructing.

Now pick up the three pennies and concentrate again on your question. Rub or roll them between your palms and fingers. Throw them a second time. Note the number of heads and tails, and write them down directly *above* the first throw.

Repeat this sequence for a total of six times. You should end up with a list that looks something like this:

(Sixth throw) two heads, one tail

(Fifth throw) three heads

(Fourth throw) three tails

(Third throw) three heads

(Second throw) two heads, one tail

(First throw) two tails, one head

## *Scoring the Coins*

Score each line by giving the value of 2 for each tail and 3 for each head. For this example, you will end up with values that look like this:

| | |
|---|---|
| (Sixth throw) two heads, one tail | 8 |
| (Fifth throw) three heads | 9 |
| (Fourth throw) three tails | 6 |
| (Third throw) three heads | 9 |
| (Second throw) two heads, one tail | 8 |
| (First throw) two tails, one head | 7 |

Now it gets a little more complicated. First the basics: Hexagrams are composed of *yin* (broken) lines and *yang* (unbroken) lines; yin lines are understood to be female, and yang lines are male (more on this later). When you throw the coins, the number 7 indicates a yang (unbroken) line, and the number 8 indicates a yin (broken) line. These are straightforward lines that easily contribute to foretelling the future, and they are drawn as follows:

——————— yang line (unbroken)
—— —— yin line (broken)

When throwing the coins, the numbers 6 and 9 indicate what are called "moving lines." The number 6 indicates a moving yin line, and 9 indicates a moving yang line. The moving lines are drawn like this:

————0———— yang moving line
————x———— yin moving line

To sum up, lines should be drawn according to the following chart:

2 tails, 1 head = 7 = yang (solid line)         ——————————
3 heads = 9 = yang (moving line)                ——————0——————
2 heads, 1 tail = 8 = yin (broken line)         ———— ————
3 tails = 6 = yin (moving line)                 ————x————

Each time you throw the coins, convert your heads and tails to lines that are either broken (yin) or solid (yang), or moving yin or yang lines. Be careful to identify each line accurately, again from the bottom up. Ask someone else to draw the lines while you do the math, if that would help.

The coin-throws in the example above would yield a hexagram that looks like this:

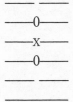

Moving lines indicate slightly different interpretations of a hexagram.

## *Identifying the Hexagram*

Next, look up the hexagram in the chart at the back of this book (page 285). You will see that each hexagram is made up of two trigrams — the bottom three lines being the lower trigram, and the top three lines being the upper trigram.

Begin by locating the first (bottom) trigram in the list on the left-hand side of the page. Next, locate the second (top) trigram along the top of the page. Trace the two lines, down and across, until you find the number that corresponds with that combination of trigrams. (This method of locating the correct hexagram is similar to finding a spot on a map by first locating the letter along the side of the map, then finding the number along the top of the map.) The hexagram thrown in the example above would be number 63, or "When You Are Done," complete with three moving lines. While no moving lines are shown in the hexagram key, adding moving lines to your drawing of the hexagram will make the predictions and instructions more reliable.

Once you have identified the hexagram's number, turn to the page that explains its meaning.

## *Interpreting the Hexagram*

Each hexagram description begins with two short epigraphs from writers who have faced a similar dilemma. It then offers a commentary, a prediction, an advisory, applicable writing exercises, and a "last word," or final advice. The writing exercises can be used immediately, and should take about a half an hour to complete.

Keep in mind that each hexagram can mean lots of different things, and even a seemingly straightforward answer can mean its opposite. Take the advice and comments with a grain of salt. Use the hexagram as a hint, rather than an unequivocal answer. Let it direct you toward thinking about your question in new ways. Taking into account the convergence of male and female lines in your hexagram, for example, might give you insight into a writing relationship in your life.

*Female and Male Lines*

Yin, or female, lines are traditionally associated with feeling, darkness, earthiness, and the moon. Yin lines are an invitation to plumb your inner world as a writer. These lines might be understood as the source of what Stephen Spender called "Beethovian" composing — thunderous writing that knows no bounds. (Of course, it is just a convention that we call such traits "female." We all know numerous women who have many of the traits ascribed to yang.)

Yang, or male, lines represent outer motivations and goals; they are often governed by reason and the sun. Spender might have called these lines "Mozartian" for their precision and formulaic structures.

The relationship between yin and yang lines in a hexagram represents the relationship between writers and readers, or writers and their work. Use your imagination as you interpret these hexagrams with growing knowledge and sophistication. Explore how the male and female lines develop the hexagram's meaning.

*Moving Lines*

If your hexagram is made up entirely of 7s and 8s, you need read no farther than For the Writer. On the other hand, if it has some 6s and 9s, you have moving lines in your hexagram. This may indicate a lack of firm form and the possibility of transition. In this book, each moving line offers a variation on the hexagram's writing exercises and advice. The topmost moving line is the most important prediction and indicates the writing exercise you should do. Ignore the other predictions and exercises suggested.

Some scholars suggest that you read the moving lines by shifting those lines to their opposite (a moving yin line becomes a solid yang line, for example), and exploring the new hexagram as another dimension to your answer.

## THE REST OF THIS BOOK

If you wish to explore further writing exercises, turn to "More Practice for the Writer" (page 247). There you will find sixty-four additional writing exercises, each one tied to a specific hexagram. You will also find a list of which exercises might be best suited for working on a particular question or dilemma.

The next section of this book, "Foxes and Deer of the Imagination," tells about how I stumbled on the topic of this book and delves into the role of imagination in writing. It also describes my revival of Carl Jung's famous experiment: throwing the I Ching to learn more about this book.

Finally, in the last section, I provide you with a short glossary of literary terms.

I wish you great fortune in using *The I Ching for Writers* to help you on your writer's path. Whether or not its oracular readings are true, they're certainly suggestive. And if you practice interpreting the commentaries and predictions as they reveal your present situation, your readings will get better with time. Ultimately this book will help you develop the interpretive skills of a prescient mind.

Stay open to the powers of the imagination, and let the ink flow.

### REVIEW

The basic steps of "throwing" the I Ching are as follows:

1.  Ask a question.

2.  "Throw" three coins six times, recording their configuration (heads or tails) from the bottom up.

3.  Add up the score for each line as follows:

    • three tails = 6

    • two tails and one head = 7

    • two heads and one tail = 8

    • three heads = 9

    Count all lines that have a 6 or a 9 as "moving lines."

4.  Draw the hexagram from the bottom up, using the following guide:

    7 = yang                    ————————
    9 = yang moving line    ————0————
    8 = yin                     ———  ———
    6 = yin moving line     ————x————

5.  Using the hexagram key at the back of the book, identify your hexagram.

6.  Turn to the hexagram indicated. Read the general hexagram commentary, prediction, and advisory. If you have any moving lines (6s or 9s), read those too. If you have more than one moving line, the topmost one is the one you should read.

# THE HEXAGRAMS

# 1. Ch'ien

*Begin Again*

*I always do the first line well,*
*but I have trouble doing the others.*

— MOLIÈRE

*I put the words down and push them a bit.*

— EVELYN WAUGH

## COMMENTARY

This is an auspicious hexagram. The six solid lines indicate yang, the sign of power, possibility, strength, and reaching for the heavens. To cast such a hexagram indicates that rewriting your beginning could be auspicious.

## PREDICTION

When you take a new approach to the project at hand, you will enjoy great success.

## ADVISORY

The advice is to start afresh. You must begin a new project, take a fresh perspective on an old one, or begin to write a piece again. Recast a poem into a new form; add another scene or act to a play; invent a new character that enters your work of fiction or creative nonfiction as a baby. Or cast the voice, point of view, plot, or character afresh.

Also, recognize that the start of any project involves indecision and fear. Relish the uncertainty. Embrace the possibilities. Face the fears head-on and rise above nagging doubts.

## FOR THE WRITER

Write from a point of view you have never tried before. You are an old man, a foreign-exchange student, a horse, a cad, an unhappy first-grader.

## MOVING LINES

Nine at the beginning means there is a hidden obstacle. Write from the point of view of a dragon.

Nine in the second place means there will be a special electric charge to your writing today. Write from the point of view of a superior, such as a boss.

Nine in the third place means there may be some danger to your writing today. Write today, if you can, while it is light outside. Write from the point of view of a magpie.

Nine in the fourth place means you will have to face

important choices today — choices that will force you to decide where to put the transitions. Write from the point of view of a creature that regularly slips between water and air (e.g., a porpoise, a turtle, a diver).

Nine in the fifth place means that your influence is spreading. Write from the point of view of a very successful writer.

Nine at the top means you have gone too far; you have lost touch with reality in your work. Write from the point of view of an ordinary person, someone you would see eating lunch in the park.

If you have cast all nines — all moving lines — it means that the whole hexagram is in motion and you will achieve strength. Continue to write in the way you have been.

## LAST WORD

As you start to write, take on one of the following challenges: begin a new friendship with another writer; create a new way of dealing with interruptions to your writing; take a short walk and end up somewhere you have never been before; make a fresh cup of tea; take a hot bath with salts, bubbles, dried milk, or oils that you have never tried before; begin, or begin again; change the subject. Seek the fresh and the new in all that you write. As the point of view of your writing changes, seek to change yourself as well.

# 2. K'UN

*Grounded Writing*

*All the soarings of my mind begin in my blood.*

— RAINER MARIA RILKE

*Art is the only thing that can go on mattering*
*once it has stopped hurting.*

— ELIZABETH BOWEN

## COMMENTARY

This hexagram is auspicious. It is rooted in the feminine
— the yin — and finds its greatest strength in earth, the
soil, the ground. Do not be afraid to face the darkness.
Creativity is strong under this sign.

## PREDICTION

If the right woman guides you, you will find your creative spirit rejuvenated.

## ADVISORY

You and your writing will grow. The darkness of yin is
fertile. It invites you to do a kind of writing that is slow,
considered, sensuous, deep. Listen to the rivers, hear the
language of the blood. Write that which is rooted in
truth, meaning, and elemental being. Seek earthy companions on the way.

## FOR THE WRITER

Paint the darkness. Use words as a flashlight.

## MOVING LINES

Six at the beginning means pay attention to the first
signs of decay in your writing. Beware writing that is
not tied to the ground. Turn your imaginary flashlight
on a stark winter scene, and find the place where hoar-
frost turns to ice. Write about that place.

Six in the second place means that you are writing
in circles. Pay more attention to balancing the creative
and the receptive. Turn your flashlight on a new scene,
one that you have never imagined before, and write.

Six in the third place means you should bring part
of your writing to a close soon. Have your writing
mature in the dark, then bring it to a close. Turn your
flashlight onto a part of a landscape where field meets
forest.

Six in the fourth place means you should write
in solitude, anonymous, away from any immediate
recognition. Hide. Turn off your flashlight and stand

wherever it leaves you. Write what you can see in the darkness.

Six in the fifth place means you will be successful in this piece of writing only if you don't talk about it; don't even mention it, unless you are asked. Maintain discretion. Turn your flashlight on yourself and note the places where vanity shows. Write about it.

Six at the top means you are not being properly receptive to the muse, the creative. Wait. Listen. Turn your flashlight onto whoever is trying to talk to you; find the creative spirit and write about that.

When all the lines are sixes, it means to endure. Turn your flashlight again on the darkness, and follow its beam no matter where it takes you. Write especially about all the obstacles ahead, noting them as obstacles you will overcome.

## LAST WORD

This hexagram indicates the earth. For writers, this means to keep the writing close to what is real. Locate the places in your poem or prose where the writing is stilted or pretentious. Weed out these phrases and any other part of the poem or story that is unconnected with reality. Beware of the tendency to write in a stilted voice to disguise your lack of knowledge. Study your topic until you could explain it to a five-year-old. Put your ear to the earth and see if you can hear what is coming.

# 3. CHUN

*Address Difficulties*

*I believe you can have constructive accidents en route
through a novel only because you have mapped a clear way
...The more you know about a book, the freer you can be to
fool around. The less you know, the tighter you get.*

— JOHN IRVING

*Great artists feel as opportunity
what others feel as menace.*

— KENNETH BURKE

## COMMENTARY

No path is without wrinkle, no friendship without difficulty, no direction always true, no relationship to writing easy and clear.

## PREDICTION

Do not avoid the pain of writing well. Then success will
be yours.

## ADVISORY

Find the path that best suits your temperament and talents, and set forth. Ignore the stumbling blocks, the gossips, the envious, the bad days, and stick to that path no matter what others may think.

## FOR THE WRITER

Look at a daily newspaper or a magazine. Find a story that involves a person facing some difficulty. Write the interior monologue (see Glossary, p. 279) of that person.

## MOVING LINES

Nine at the beginning means you will be beset by difficulties. Friends or other writing companions can help. Find a story in the newspaper about a disaster, and write a short piece of advice for people who find themselves in such a jam.

Six in the second place means that problems with writing pile up, and you have trouble proceeding. Do not accept help now, however kindly offered. Find a story in your newspaper or magazine that features a person beset by grave difficulties. Write a short account of someone offering help to that person and being refused.

Six in the third place means that if you try too hard, you will be humiliated. Give up on some immediate goal and instead endure through the problems ahead. Read the newspaper or magazine until you find a story of a person in harm's way. Write about how that person might overcome that harm by doing nothing.

Six in the fourth place means that we must act, while carefully conserving the limited energy we have. Take the first step toward a solution. Write about a person in the newspaper or magazine who is persevering against all odds.

Nine in the fifth place means to be steady in your writing. Push yourself to generate new work, but do not push yourself too hard. Take a look at your newspaper or magazine and write a flash fiction (see Glossary, p. 278) about a photograph you see.

Six at the top means that grave dangers lie ahead in your life as a writer. Do not travel; stay close to home. Be steady and clear, and do not persist in a path that goes nowhere. Read an obituary or account of someone's life in your newspaper or magazine. Consider what it means to be vulnerable. Write out some suggestions to yourself about how to survive this immediate danger to you or your manuscript.

## LAST WORD

Be clear in conversations; exercise your conviction at all costs. Address difficulties in your art, in reaction to your art, and in the process by which you create your art. Be open and clear. Say what you think. Write what you feel. Beware the difficulties to come, but be honest. By all means, keep yourself safe in the face of unspecified dangers.

# 4. MÊNG

*Embracing Darkness*

*A good novel is possible
only after one has given up and let go.*

— WALKER PERCY

*I knew it seemed impossible for me to write in the
traditional forms. They seemed to have no access
to what we experienced. If we enclosed that in characters,
personalities, a plot, we were overlooking everything
that our senses were perceiving.*

— NATHALIE SARRAUTE

## COMMENTARY

You are used to seeking insight in the full glare of the sun. Now you must turn your back on the light and go deep within the world of the self. Do not ignore the animus, the dark side of self that is generative and wise and bold. Let loose your creative energy that may at first seem too primitive or instinctual. Find the darkness within you and let it into your stories, your poems, your characters, all the writing you do. Be young, and even a little foolish, as you explore your writing afresh.

## PREDICTION

If you seek what is dark in your writing and let it express itself, your poems and stories will be the source of real brilliance, for you and your readers.

## ADVISORY

Admit those hopes that are dangerous or gloomy; admit those feelings that are in disrepute. Let your voice within your writing be full and round, articulating the dusk. Do not be afraid of self, of the sky when no moon shows. Find the dark truths that lie beneath the cobwebs.

## FOR THE WRITER

Write a poem that is a dramatic monologue (see Glossary, p. 277) from the point of view of a very young character who is about to kill another, older character — but doesn't know it yet.

## MOVING LINES

Six at the beginning means that to continue in this vein will lead to real foolhardiness. You are acting too young and need discipline. Write a short poem about an accident with a gun.

Nine in the second place means to be kind to your own foolish, dark tendencies. Replace those tendencies with resolution and mature vision — but be gentle. Write a short poem about a contemporary version of "the boy who cried wolf."

Six in the third place means you should not throw yourself after a teacher who has not offered to advise you. Come to terms with your own darkness alone. Write a short poem about a girl who, in her youthful foolishness and lack of clarity, throws herself at another person.

Six in the fourth place means to pull back from foolish imaginings. Get your feet back on the ground, and do not be attracted only to the mysteries of the darkness. Grow up. Write a short poem about an immature boy who has an experience that forces him to maturity.

Six in the fifth place means you will find a way through, simply by being yourself. Stay in touch with the darkness inside you, and do not fight it. Write a short poem about a girl who wakes up to the idea that she can survive the darkness all around her by simply being herself.

Nine at the top means you will be punished for not observing the correct approach to darkness. Your only hope is to restore an intelligent order to your work. Write a short poem about your own work to date, concentrating on what changes you can make to it that both acknowledge the darkness and bring order to it.

## LAST WORD

Who are you when you write? What do you do in that state? Who can you talk to when the drawbridge won't go down, the casino has taken all your money, your car has no brakes, and you are speeding toward the edge? As a writer, you need to embrace the darkness that is already there, finding truth in a mirror that shows darkness all around your reflection. Seek a wise teacher.

# 5. Hsü

*Pause*

*The daydreamer, the procrastinator, the flaneur —
these are people who understand the pace of writing.
Writers know the white space between words, the
pause between each beat of the heart. They know that
sometimes they need time to do nothing more than
contemplate their own breathing and dream.*

— SARAH JANE SLOANE

*. . . we ourselves are like a very sensitive
engraving plate, and we don't know what marks us.
In fact, everything marks us in a way.*

— EDMOND JABÈS

## COMMENTARY

You are moving too fast through the world. You are in
too much of a hurry as you seek recognition and success.
Pause. Look inside yourself. Are you doing all you can
to make yourself feel nourished? Stop right where you
are and appraise the situation.

## PREDICTION

If you continue to work at such a breakneck speed, you will not find the graceful solitude that you need when you compose.

## ADVISORY

Be honest with yourself. You must pause and breathe deep, letting the air enter the arches of your feet, both hands, and the crown of your head, circulating through your entire body. Ask yourself what you need to realize your most creative self. Ask yourself the way home, the way to your real home, the place where your body and soul feel alive. Ask yourself what you must do to find equanimity on your path to becoming a writer.

## FOR THE WRITER

Draw a picture of the writer inside you. Look at the picture for a while, then write what it would say to you if it could truly speak.

## MOVING LINES

Nine at the beginning means to stay still, exactly where you are, and no harm will come. Do not waste your strength on unnecessary struggle. Write a description of yourself as a writer who waits, meditates, stays cool and calm no matter what arrives.

Nine in the second place means there may be some mean-spirited gossip about you. Do not honor it by responding. Write a portrait of yourself as a writer who ignores all idle words spoken around (or about) you.

Nine in the third place means that to wait too long is to invite sloth, hesitation, or worry to arrive. While staying still and calm is beneficial, to stay that way for too long is to lose ground. Write a short sketch of yourself as a writer who awakens and takes action.

Six in the fourth place means that the situation around you is extremely dangerous. The only way out of this danger is to wait, to be still and calm. Imagine yourself sitting cross-legged in a very peaceful surrounding. Watch your own breath come and go. Write a short piece about yourself in this posture. Stay still.

Nine in the fifth place means that there will be peace for you if you continue on this path. Not all will be peace in the long run, but for now you will find contentment. Imagine yourself as a writer walking through desolate hills (e.g., Wyoming or Alaska). Write about what it means to be someone who has found peace through writing steadily and well.

Six at the top means that danger has already arrived. It is no longer avoidable. But to help you escape the danger, aid from an unexpected source will arrive. Write a self-portrait of you as a writer overcoming the toughest challenges of your work.

## LAST WORD

Think back to the last time when you were truly relaxed. What were you doing? Who were you with? Check in on your shoulders even as you read this. Are they scrunched up and tight? Observe your breathing. Is it shallow or deep? Take a little time every day to culti-vate calm and stillness, to nourish the writer inside you. Feed the imagination; rest the body; clear the mind. Meditate on what gives your life real meaning.

# 6. SUNG

## *Writing Dangerously*

*I think a little menace is fine to have in a story.*
*For one thing, it's good for the circulation.*

— RAYMOND CARVER

*I like to write when I feel spiteful; it's like a good sneeze.*

— D. H. LAWRENCE

### COMMENTARY

This hexagram suggests taking risks in writing. Let your characters go places they wouldn't ordinarily go. All is ultimately empty, all is impermanent. Fire licks the edges of reality. That which we think has substance today will be ash tomorrow.

### PREDICTION

Being too careful leads backward. When you step forward, you will skate across the abyss and learn your real name.

## ADVISORY

Introduce fire into your poems and stories — the literal image of flames licking buildings, trees, crates, anything flammable. Have a character burn up some papers in whatever you are writing. Have someone in your story make love to someone she isn't supposed to. Write as though no one will ever see what you dare to say. Write as though you were already dead. Stop being so careful in your poems, prose, and plays.

## FOR THE WRITER

A publishing company says it will publish your science fiction, but it needs another fifty pages in less than two weeks. Write the first two pages of this section, perhaps a robot's inner monologue.

## MOVING LINES

Six at the beginning means to stop your diffident writing and throw caution to the wind. In the end, such a strategy will yield the best work. Write two pages in a genre (see Glossary, p. 278) that you don't usually explore (e.g., science fiction, love story, thriller, western). Write it quickly.

Nine in the second place means you should not give up your cautious writing. If you retreat from writing dangerously, you will benefit your readers. Write for a short time in your usual voice, in your usual form.

Six in the third place means that although writing dangerously is just that — a matter of taking real risks

— in the end you will succeed. Good luck prevails. Write something very short, perhaps half a page, that tells a secret you keep from everyone. Avoid talking to your boss, if you have one.

Nine in the fourth place means that you throw up your hands and give yourself up to whatever karma may be yours. You give up trying to control that which is ultimately fate's dominion. Write one page in poetry or prose, letting eternal principles guide your writing process.

Nine in the fifth place means that you must seek a mediator to help you negotiate between writing dangerously and writing cautiously. Such a mediator could be a person, but more likely will be an aspect of yourself. Write a page in which you weigh the pros and cons of writing in the two different patterns.

Nine at the top means you have triumphed in your attempts to write dangerously. However, the conflict is not over. Pause and write two pages about you celebrating a temporary victory over the most cautious aspects of your writing.

## LAST WORD

Don't be so cautious in your writing. Skate closer to the edge. When you write, wear clothes that make you feel dangerous. Let your characters run toward conflict, embrace contention. Put them in traps and places they can't escape. Stop being so careful with your poems and prose.

# 7. Shih

*Be Strong*

*Writing is an intellectual process, so it is good to root the process into your stomach, your heart, your bowels.*

— MARIA IRENE FORNES

*Every woman who writes is a survivor.*

— SUSAN GRIFFIN

## COMMENTARY

This is both an auspicious sign and a warning. When all forces are arrayed against you, you can run and hide or you can face adversity squarely. Both stances are appropriate at different times. This hexagram does not prescribe which stance to take, but it suggests that however you meet conflict, you must learn to show strength.

## PREDICTION

An unexpected setback will affect your work. When you show real strength of character in the face of this disappointment, the setback will be transformed into something more positive.

## ADVISORY

It is easy to appear strong as you face off with the blank page day after day. However, any writer knows the difficulty of maintaining discipline and confidence in the craft of writing. Every writer knows that no past success guarantees future accomplishment. Look deep inside yourself and realize that being square with yourself is the most important source of strength. Write the story you know you should be writing, not that which is easiest or best pleases the crowd. Persevere.

## FOR THE WRITER

Write a story in the style of magic realism (see Glossary, p. 280) about an old woman who keeps praying for salvation.

## MOVING LINES

Six at the beginning means you must be orderly as well as strong. Develop discipline in your writing habits. Write in the style of magic realism about an old man who has followed the same routine for over forty years.

Nine in the second place means you must be a strong writer, not only for yourself but for others who write also — whether in your writing group or for strangers who write. You must inspire by example. Write a page or two in the style of magic realism, in which you describe a magical cat.

Six in the third place means bad luck, unless you lead others strongly. If you are in a writers' group, coordinate its exercises this time; if you are writing for publication, write a strong and persuasive query letter. Write a page or two in the style of magic realism about a haunted house; erase no single word; let your first draft be your last draft because you get it almost right the first time.

Six in the fourth place means to remember that there are times to be weak as well as times to be strong. Bend with the wind. Write one or two pages in the style of magic realism, in which you retreat from strength in your writing and instead let yourself slide back into a more familiar genre (see Glossary, p. 278); the topic of your writing should be an army in retreat.

Six in the fifth place means there are images that you know already that you can use in your writing. Go back and look at what you have written, and circle those parts that seem fertile. Write a page or two in the style of magic realism, in which you use those phrases, lines, or sections afresh, creating the first two pages of a tale about an eldest son leading a group of ragtag soldiers.

Six at the top means that you should not settle for inferior characters or lines of poetry and prose. You must be ruthless in choosing what words or passages to delete. Write a page or two in the style of magic realism about a cow that doesn't give milk. Then go back and take out every adverb or adjective.

## LAST WORD

Strength is always relative. You may not feel strong because you are surrounded by insurmountable tasks or by people who are stronger than you. But each of us is born with the capacity to cope with the experience given to us. Each of us should recognize this life as an opportunity to practice equanimity, to see that the greatest strength is to recognize our weakness and not mind it.

# 8. PI

*Seek Harmony in the Whole*

*I don't know why these images, which apparently spring
from the disorder of the spirit, become ordered...*

— JEAN-CLAUDE CARRIÈRE

*It is a violence from within that protects us from
a violence without. It is the imagination pressing
back against the pressure of reality.*

— WALLACE STEVENS

## COMMENTARY

At the moment, all might seem chaotic, foggy, lost. The
trick in this dim light is to hold together, to seek harmony in the whole, even when all around you is disorder, dismay, and disarray. Remember the absolute
necessity of compromise in friendship, in love, and even
in editing one's own work. Balance the attention you
pay to both content and form.

## PREDICTION

If you can let go of fantasies of self-importance and indispensability, you shall see again the fabric of the whole.

## ADVISORY

When hearing comments about your own work, try to be gracious. Take heart in your native abilities, persistence, and clarity. Know that friends and editors, even with their good intentions, sometimes miss what you are trying to say.

## FOR THE WRITER

Write a rhyming poem in which family members grow closer after the death of one of them.

## MOVING LINES

Six at the beginning means to write truthfully no matter who is your audience. Sincerity is the key to success. Think about your own family and write a poem in which you talk about how they have come to terms with a death.

Six in the second place means to write with dignity. If you write with dignity, you will please your readers. Write a poem about a person who shuns the easy way to advance in his or her career, and who relies on his or her own abilities and strengths to gain notice instead.

Six in the third place means that you are trying to please the wrong people. Force of habit brings you there. Write a poem addressed to another group of people — maybe even a group you don't know much about. This group seeks real writing, not easy flattery. Write about a conflict within your family.

Six in the fourth place means that if you persevere along the path you have chosen, you will have success as a writer. But you must persevere with seriousness and attention to your readers. Write a poem in which family members argue about ways to read poetry or prose. Step into the poem yourself toward the end, and talk about what you seek to do for your readers.

Nine in the fifth place means you must have great sympathy for yourself, a condition that will lead to good fortune. You must let yourself off the hook. When you hunt for the goodness in yourself, let it manifest with the clarity and imagination that is already there. Write a short poem about a family that meditates together every Tuesday morning and slowly realizes their innate goodness.

Six at the top means you will have great difficulty with the beginning of your work. If the beginning is not right, nothing will be right in your work. Take your time and go back to the beginning, recasting your words so that you make a solid start. Then write a poem in which you meditate on the qualities of a good beginning — in your writing, in a class, on a job, or in a relationship — and then apply that poem's insights to your own work.

## LAST WORD

Softening the heart and gaining equilibrium, especially in the face of physical or psychological disorder, is hard work. But it is necessary work. You must attempt to no longer blame others for the disorder of your life or your writing. You must put one foot in front of the other, slow though it may be, and work hard to bring the chaos into order.

# 9. Hsiao Ch'u

## *Pay Attention to the Details*

*I never thought of it as a poem, I thought of it as lines that just didn't happen to go all the way across the page.*

— E. L. DOCTOROW

*I am not a solitary man and I suffer greatly
from spending eight or nine or ten hours
a day sitting alone, hunched, drawing a hump,
and scribbling little fly's feet on white paper...*

— CARLOS FUENTES

### COMMENTARY

The devil is in the details, and it is the details that count the most. One of the most meticulous novelists said that a writer should know every object in a room he is describing, all the way down to the doorknobs. Pay attention to the smallest details. Remember the bit characters, the side plots, the bouquet of cheap carnations and a single sprig of baby's breath on the kitchen table.

## PREDICTION

You will write the rough draft of an excellent creative work whose full value will not be revealed until you add the details. If you nurture the small parts of the story (or poem), the end result will be very successful.

## ADVISORY

Take your time as you write. Close your eyes and imagine every person, every detail, every prop, every thought. Give yourself enough time to write a single scene. And when you revise, be sure to give every line the close attention it deserves.

## FOR THE WRITER

Ask a friend to mail you a postcard with an interesting picture on it every day for a week. When you receive each postcard, devote half an hour to writing a poem about it. Pay close attention to every detail. Or cut a picture out of a magazine and describe it so carefully that someone who has never seen it can imagine it perfectly.

## MOVING LINES

Nine at the beginning means that you should return to your usual way of writing. You can pay attention to the details later. Find seven pictures in your home and write rapidly about each one. Pay little attention to the details and much attention to the feeling of each picture.

Nine in the second place means that you should return to paying reasonable attention to detail. Behave more like the other writers you know. Find seven pictures in your home and write a short, free-verse poem (see Glossary, p. 278) about each one. Pay attention to the details, but no more than usual. If you do this, good fortune will follow.

Nine in the third place means there is real risk to your writing if you do not pay close and total attention to details. You may think that your work requires you to just press ahead, but if you do so it will be like wagon wheels trying to roll forward without any spokes. Find a central image in your own work-in-progress. Add meticulous detail, being as thorough as you possibly can. Now do this again with another image. And so on.

Six in the fourth place means to write with utmost sincerity while paying attention to the details. Write from the heart. Find seven pictures and let each one trigger a personal truth. Write down that truth, noting the details of its circumstance. Fear not the raw statement, the blunt assertion, the frank confidence.

Nine in the fifth place means that you are rich in knowing people, or perhaps just one partner, who can help you with your writing. Trust these friends to tell you the truth about your writing. Find seven pictures and write from the point of view of a person or object in each one. Have some fun with this game. Show your writing to your helpful friends and share your pleasure.

Nine at the top means success is nearly yours, but do not advance further. Wait for the moment of final achievement to arrive on its own; do not force anything.

Find seven pictures and describe the darkness of image or character in each one. Write in a gloomy tone. However, do not press ahead by adding such details to your own writing. Free write (see Glossary, p. 278) instead about your work-in-progress.

## LAST WORD

Think about what it means to be small. What are the parts of your world that are small? Who is overlooked in your home? Why do we not notice the smallest parts of the natural world? Next time you have a chance, take a very slow walk and notice the smallest objects or plants you see. Thoroughly describe them in your writer's notebook.

# 10. LÜ

## *Find the Writer's Path*

*A writer has the duty to be good, not lousy; true, not false; lively, not dull; accurate, not full of error. He should tend to lift people up, not lower them down. Writers do not merely reflect and interpret life, they inform and shape life.*

— E. B. WHITE

*The imagination loses vitality as it ceases to adhere to what is real.*

— WALLACE STEVENS

## COMMENTARY

This hexagram suggests you think of yourself as a writer, which is itself a dramatic challenge. But it is exactly that challenge you must meet. According to this hexagram, you are a writer — someone who is serious about his or her writing. You must find the path to expressing that intention, that talent, that work.

## PREDICTION

If you continue writing day after day, you will find yourself to be a writer. If you walk through the world imagining how you will put it into words, you will find yourself to be a writer. The day when you will call yourself a writer and make writing your full-time occupation is closer than you think.

## ADVISORY

Take your life's work very seriously. Go through a day with compassion in your heart and a desire to use language fairly and carefully at all times. Do not forget the importance of a well-chosen silence.

## FOR THE WRITER

Make a list of everything you need to be at your most creative. Then choose the most important three, and write about how you can find them in your present life.

## MOVING LINES

Nine at the beginning means that the writer's path is a simple one. Do not force it, do not work so hard to find it. Simply live it. Write a deeply felt poem in which you muse about what the writer's path might look like. In the poem, put yourself on that path and tell your readers what you see.

Nine in the second place means that the writer's path is smooth, easy, and calm, once you find it. To be a writer does not mean to suffer and drink and despair. Write a portrait of a writer as you imagine him or her. Now imagine that writer as a healthy person.

Six in the third place means that you may misunderstand your conception of yourself. You may not sufficiently understand the writer's path and may leap ahead, too arrogant to understand its nuance or simplicity. Write a short poem in which you stop in your tracks and write about what it means to be a writer on your path. Be humble.

Nine in the fourth place means to be cautious in trying to find the writer's path. Do not hurry or tread on the tiger's tail; that way is dangerous. Write a page or two in which you describe either a writer in real danger or the dangerous traits of a writer.

Nine in the fifth place means that you will carry on despite obvious signs of danger. You will be resolute, but not so resolute as to miss what is really going on. Write a page or two in which you describe the dangers of success for a writer following the writer's path.

Nine at the top means to examine your own heart for the answer to the riddle *What is the writer's path?* When that answer arrives with truth and sincerity, good fortune is guaranteed. Write two or three pages in which you are utterly honest in describing what is the path of a writer, especially when that writer is you.

### LAST WORD

Plotting the writer's path in a world grown increasingly dangerous and worrisome is no easy task. Once you have swept away distraction, focused on your task, and written 600 words or more in a day, you will find yourself a writer. More than any other qualities, a writer must have confidence and persistence. Both are necessary. When you set your pen upon the page, it is crucial to remember that all writers began the same way. Have confidence. Your job is to do the work, to believe in the work, to persist in the work. Then you will be a writer.

# 11. T'AI

*Write in Peace and Quiet*

*I often see many stars early in the morning. The stars are nothing but the light which has traveled at great speed many miles from the heavenly bodies. But for me the stars are not speedy beings, but calm, steady, and peaceful beings...There is harmony in our activity, and where there is harmony there is calmness.*

— SHUNRYU SUZUKI

*If the mind is comely, everything that mind produces is comely.*

— LAWRENCE FERLINGHETTI

## COMMENTARY

Slow down. There is no real hurry. No rush, no noise, no deadlines. Today is your day to take long, slow strides in your writing. Understand your poems and stories about the world as simple, graceful, true. Write in peace and quiet, and you will do your very best work. This hexagram connotes success, good fortune, great joy in observations of everything from great stars to tiny insects.

## PREDICTION

You will soon understand the sheer necessity of calm in your writing. You will find your way, after trial and error, to being centered and settled, quiet and secure. Your imagination will roam without distraction and you will find an impressive truth — about yourself and your writing.

## ADVISORY

Not only should you be calm, but your characters or lyrics should embrace stillness. Find ways to allow your readers to pause in the dance, to halt the whirlwind of distracting thoughts. Suspense grows best for your reader when you write in the quiet of dawn or the silences of deep night. Be still.

## FOR THE WRITER

Describe in detail a single footstep of your postal carrier. Pay attention to pacing (see Glossary, p. 280), sound, the visual detail of the shoe. What socks is he or she wearing? How scuffed is the shoe? Is the footstep peaceful or anxious? Write slowly and methodically about this close observation.

## MOVING LINES

Nine at the beginning means that like-minded people are joining your party. You are connected with a wide range of other writers. Write a page in which you describe the shoes of three mail carriers. Use five-sense imagery (see Glossary, p. 278) creatively: "The third pair of shoes was worn at the heel. A light scent of shoe polish rose from the shiny toes, and his socks were the color of an old anger."

Nine in the second place means that you should be gentle with your companions. Walk the middle way, and beware of too much prosperity. Write a page in which you describe the shoes of a postal carrier who is down on his luck, has an imperfect delivery style, and is the kind of man who is more likely to walk through a puddle than around it.

Nine in the third place means that all is impermanent. Everything you are or know is subject to change. Write a page in which you describe the postal carrier's shoes from three perspectives: what do they look like now; what did they look like in their past; and what will they look like in their future? Use very specific imagery.

Six in the fourth place means do not brag about your accomplishments. Be sincere. Write a page or more about a very wealthy postal clerk who sits behind a desk and sells stamps simply because he wants to. What do his shoes look like? What indicates his wealth in his socks or shoes? Practice revealing character through details of clothing.

Six in the fifth place means that high and low unite and good will is created. Happiness is fostered. Write a page in which you describe the shoes of two mail carriers who have fallen in love.

Six at the top means you should beware of violence. Persistence against an enemy is futile. Maintain good community. Write a page or two about a community of postal workers who are having their annual meeting during a blizzard. Have them show some camaraderie as the snow floats overhead.

## LAST WORD

Writing in peace is different from writing cautiously. According to this hexagram, it is still necessary to take risks and make quick cuts. But afterwards you must return to the center of your stillness. There is the dance, and then the pause in the dance. This hexagram invokes the pause.

# 12. P'I

*Obstacles Are Opportunities*

*No tears in the writer, no tears in the reader.*

— ROBERT FROST

*Nothing is pointless, and nothing is meaningless if the artist will face it. And it's his business to face it.*

— KATHERINE ANNE PORTER

## COMMENTARY

This is both an auspicious sign and one that signals trouble. It suggests perseverance as much as it does transformation. Forces will conspire to bring your writing to a halt. Work through that obstacle and you will find that it ultimately improves your writing.

## PREDICTION

Larger concerns threaten to take over your day's writing time. Steadily approach the day's dangers and stay the course.

## ADVISORY

Walk slowly and steadily through the threats to your creativity today. Don't be daunted. Mistrust seems to prevail everywhere, but you must trust your own instincts to the end. Let no person or distraction get in the way of your creativity today. Balance your responsibilities to the larger world and to your own work with grace and certitude.

## FOR THE WRITER

Write five haiku (see Glossary, p. 279), one about each room in your house — or any house you know well. For each room, identify a problem with the room (an object out of place, for example, or a problem with noise or the room's feng shui, ambience, or view) or a problem with the way you feel in that room.

## MOVING LINES

Six at the beginning means that success will come when you retire from battle. You will spare yourself humiliation by knowing when to persevere and when to leave. Write five haiku about leaving.

Six in the second place means that success is not far away. The inferior will prosper but the great will grow even greater. Write five linked haiku that follow the career of a single person. Have that person grow progressively more successful in each haiku.

Six in the third place means shame. This shame comes from not being up to the work being asked of you. Write five linked haiku that follow the career of a single person heading downwards. Have that person grow progressively more feeble in each haiku.

Nine in the fourth place means that you must respond only to your higher calling. If you respond to that calling, everything else will fall into place. Write five haiku about celestial beings, the supernal creatures that may speak to us if only we will listen.

Nine in the fifth place means that you can no longer stand still. You must initiate a change. Write five haiku in which you play with a single image — a tree, a cat, a lake, or a camera, for example — and have that image appear and be transformed in each successive haiku.

Nine at the top means that you have quit standing still, so you may achieve good fortune. You now know the difference between stillness and stagnation. Write five haiku about yourself as you are about to embark on a journey.

## LAST WORD

Your creative process must be nurtured. It will constantly be overshadowed by the day's duties, the momentum of the mundane, the tempo of recurring responsibilities. You must carve out time for your imagination, overcoming distractions and negative or self-defeating thoughts. Be creative, be true to yourself, even if occasionally at the cost of others.

# 13. T'UNG JÊN

*Be Aware of the Creative Voices Inside You*

*But ponder as well the deep symbolic shifts
that are forming beneath your consciousness,
and of which you are the voice.*

— WILLIAM EVERSON

*They should be ones whose hearts are easily broken
and who have so many characters in their heads
they should charge them rent.*

— LESLEE BECKER

## COMMENTARY

This hexagram indicates creativity's flux. The creative process involves listening out of the stillness that is your mind's natural state. Once you are still, settled, grounded, you may see characters, hear their voices, be able to run after them with a pencil in your hand. Keep your focus on your interior — those private thoughts and feelings that frame your essential character.

## PREDICTION

Listen well, trust your instincts, and success is at hand.

## ADVISORY

The advice here is to drop everything and be still. Then turn your attention to the inner landscape and listen to what is said from that place. Don't judge. Don't edit or revise. Simply listen to the suggestions that feed your writing process. Then write down those suggestions.

## FOR THE WRITER

Write down the first dream you can remember ever having. Then write down the most recent dream you can remember. Write a flash fiction (see Glossary, p. 278) using either dream as a jumping off point.

## MOVING LINES

Nine at the beginning means no secrets. Make friends, proceed as you normally would, and all will be fine. Remember a dream that you had recently. Tell the dream from the point of view of an object in the dream. For example, if you dreamed of a bedroom, tell the dream from the point of view of the bed.

Six in the second place means humiliation. You will be in danger of forming an exclusive group — a clique or a faction — that will scorn other groups in order to make itself feel grand. Avoid this arrangement. Write a couple of pages of prose about any nightmare, especially a recurring nightmare, that you have had.

Nine in the third place means that you essentially mistrust your own creativity. Listen better to your instincts. Free write (see Glossary, p. 278) a couple of pages about what you dream.

Nine in the fourth place means that sadness will turn to joy. You will learn how to trust your own creative voices and to write more freely. Write about a nightmare you once had and then rewrite the nightmare into a good dream.

Nine in the fifth place means that laughter will follow discomfort. Don't take yourself or your creativity too seriously. Write a page or two about a funny dream — make one up, if you like, or write down a real one.

Nine at the top means that you recognize your own creativity, but you don't connect to it fully enough. You must connect your own creativity to who you really are. Write a page or two about a dream you wish you had realized.

## LAST WORD

The trick is to listen and write. Your imagination is fertile, fecund, ready to reveal. Your task is to give it stillness and space so that it can reveal itself. Find the people who live in your mind. Give each one of them a chance to talk. Listen well.

# 14. TA YU

*Acknowledge a Great Vision
That You Already Possess*

*A fiction writer's attitude, generally referred to as an author's
"vision," is what informs and gives meaning, especially moral
meaning, to the plot, the form and structure of the narrative,
the point of view, and the characters; it gives meaning even
to the tiniest detail, to the sheen, if singled out, reflected off
the dewy surface of a single oak leaf at dawn.*

— RUSSELL BANKS

*Poetry is the art of understanding what it is to be alive.*

— ARCHIBALD MACLEISH

## COMMENTARY

Choosing this hexagram is propitious and reveals that
you already have a great vision for your work. Now you
must clarify it, carry it forward. Many visions are fleeting or partial, unclear, uninspired. In contrast, this hexagram acknowledges your talent and clarity, the fact that
you know exactly what must happen. If you have any
question at all, it is about how to implement this grand
vision. The vision itself is not in question.

## PREDICTION

You shall remember the overall shape and purpose of your writing, and that memory will yield a new and rich approach. You should be confident about your efforts to write important work.

## ADVISORY

You must dig into your writing after remembering its deepest impulse. Find your way back home to the fecund gardens of the imagination. Listen to the thrum of your heart and vision. Remember what you are trying to do, and then do it.

## FOR THE WRITER

Find a photograph of yourself and study it. Where are you headed? Where are your eyes looking? Then write down what the photograph doesn't show: your mood, your thoughts, your dreams. Pay attention to your inner vision.

## MOVING LINES

Nine at the beginning means there is nothing harmful around you. Your vision is strong and unencumbered. Write a short poem in which you describe what you see inside yourself, what that inner truth might be.

Nine in the second place means you are free of mistakes. Everything is fine. Proceed as you have been, writing a journal entry about your life's course. What vision is guiding you now?

Nine in the third place means not to be greedy. Share your possessions with others, especially with someone more important than you. Write a poem in which you describe and explain your relationship to one material possession.

Nine in the fourth place means you should not be envious of others' visions. You may find yourself walking among the rich and famous, and you should not let them throw you off course. Write a poem that describes how you look to others, both inside and outside.

Six in the fifth place means that you will have very good fortune. Your sincerity wins over all sorts of people. Write a poem from the very center of your heart about some truth you believe.

Nine at the top means that you should be both modest and true. It is sometimes a difficult balancing act. Think of some aspect of your life for which you are grateful. Write a short poem in which you talk in your own voice about this aspect.

## LAST WORD

This hexagram lights up your whole inner world and reminds you of the necessary vision, the angels or dakinis or bions or photons or streaks of light that illuminate the path. Your vision brings order and intelligence to a sometimes seemingly random world. If you are true to your own vision, you shall find your way to a magnificent, resonant conclusion.

# 15. CH'IEN

*Develop a Humble Attitude*

*Never think you alone write a story.*
*You work with a combination of your own talents,*
*your characters' powers, and sheer good luck.*

— JUDY DOENGES

*There's a very thin line that separates the strong,*
*true, bright bird of the imagination from the*
*synthetic, noisy bauble.*

— ARUNDHATI ROY

## COMMENTARY

We all find ourselves in situations where we are inclined to inflate our accomplishments. This hexagram advises us to practice humility instead. Being truly humble is a way to get in touch with the real depths of the creative process. Look inside yourself and ruthlessly root out those parts of you that brag about your ability as a writer. Be sane and calm, quiet inside yourself.

## PREDICTION

You will not succeed in your writing if you continue to brag about your accomplishments.

## ADVISORY

Proceed quietly, like a fox, and let your work garner the glory, not you. Always resist the impulse to tell others about the supreme importance of your work. Proceed slowly, purposefully, quietly, and especially modestly.

## FOR THE WRITER

Find an overcoat in your house. Put it on while you write. Write a flash fiction (see Glossary, p. 278) that uses the overcoat in winter as a symbol of humility.

## MOVING LINES

Six at the beginning means you should undertake all tasks as quietly and simply as you can. Do not make a big deal out of them. Write a flash fiction about a clerk satisfied with his work.

Six in the second place means that you should behave with great modesty in all things. If you are modest, your mind will clear. Write a flash fiction about a Buddhist monk who learns something unexpected as he meditates.

Nine in the third place means a secret is disclosed. A person who is not modest will draw criticism and difficulty into his or her life. Write a flash fiction in which a man has trouble with a dog. The dog reveals a secret about the man.

Six in the fourth place means you should pay attention to the proper attitude in all things. Do not overdo modesty or taunt those who are inferior to you. Write a flash fiction in which one person robs another.

Six in the fifth place means not to boast. Instead, however, it is important to take action where action is required. Write a one-page list of instructions for someone who is trying to find a girlfriend.

Six at the top means don't blame others for your own mistakes. Take responsibility and you will find order and inspiration in your work. Write a flash fiction in which two boys get in trouble.

## LAST WORD

Taking on the proper humble attitude sometimes causes us to be overlooked or forgotten. But such aspects of humility are laudable. Our culture thrives on the boast — blowhards bragging as loud as they can. Assuming the opposite stance is of prime importance to your work as a writer.

# 16. YÜ

## *Enthusiasm*

*First and foremost, writing poems should be a pleasure.*

— PHILIP LARKIN

*If writing is going to have any effect on people morally,
it ought to affect the writer morally. It is important
to support everyone who tries to write
because their victories are your victories.*

— KEN KESEY

## COMMENTARY

This hexagram suggests that you adjust your attitude and recognize the purity and joy all around you. Greet the dawn with enthusiasm; meet the darkness with care. However, you don't necessarily have to express your enthusiasm in public. Simply feel it inside you: clear as the sky, firm as a rock. When you feel a natural enthusiasm (literally, being possessed), those all around you will also have good feelings.

## PREDICTION

You will soon feel that enthusiasm is a natural and necessary response to the joys of reading and writing.

## ADVISORY

Be aware of the challenges of creating good and evil characters, moods, tones, expressions in your writing. Your enthusiasm should be mostly directed at the good, the realization that there is strength and courage in writing solidly. Be enthusiastic when the work warrants it. Feelings of pure joy are rare in the composing process, so enjoy them to the core when they do arrive.

## FOR THE WRITER

Think of the etymology of the word "enthusiasm," its roots in "inspired by a god" or "possessed." When has enthusiasm ever "possessed" you? In a love affair, the onset of travel, the hope for a particular outcome? Write an autobiographical statement about a time when you felt possessed or inspired by the gods of enthusiasm.

## MOVING LINES

Six at the beginning means that your enthusiasm should not be expressed publicly. Be steady within yourself, and keep your enthusiastic responses to yourself. Think of a time when you were confronted by someone insufferably arrogant, and write a page or two about that person and your response.

Six in the second place means that you have real insight into when to express enthusiasm and when to keep a lower profile. Be aware of the right moment to arrive and the moment to go. Write a short autobiographical statement about a time when you stayed somewhere longer than you should have — and felt the consequences.

Six in the third place means you must act immediately. When enthusiasm for a project or a person arrives, seize the moment and express it. Write a short piece about a time when you felt marvelously enthusiastic about meeting someone.

Nine in the fourth place means you have no doubts and no fears. You draw people to you through your confidence in the quality of your projects. Write a short autobiographical piece about a moment when you felt supremely confident.

Six in the fifth place means your enthusiasm is constantly being obstructed — but by what is not clear. Such obstruction, however, is not necessarily bad since it prevents you from wasting energy on sometimes empty enthusiasms. Write a short piece about a time when you felt that a dream of yours was quashed.

Six at the top means your enthusiasm is deluded. You do not see things as they really are. Write a short autobiographical piece about a time when you were lied to and didn't realize it.

## LAST WORD

This hexagram shows thunder above and earth below.
All enthusiasms spring from stable ground and dissipate
in a volatile sky. As you explore the moments of enthusiasm that you feel as you write, be sure not to lose the
ground under your feet.

# 17. Sui

*Follow the Writer's Path*

*He would be a poet who could impress the winds
and streams into his service to speak for him; who nailed
words to their primitive senses, as farmers drive down
stakes in the spring [when the frost has first heaved]; who
derived his words as often as he used them, transplanted
them to his page with earth adhering to their roots.*

— H. D. THOREAU

*After I had written about a novel's worth of bad pages,
I understood that while I was not doing it well,
that was the thing I was going to do.*

— JOHN BARTH

## COMMENTARY

This hexagram assumes that you have found the path to
becoming a writer. Now the I Ching is recommending
that you follow such a correct path, the road that opens
before you. Such following is beneficial because you are
in the company of countless other creative spirits walking
the same road.

## PREDICTION

You will find the way and follow the path.

## ADVISORY

Stay the course. Firmness of purpose and character are necessary to keep to the writer's path. Throwing this hexagram indicates that you have both kinds of firmness.

## FOR THE WRITER

Draw a map of an imaginary country. Put some detail into the effort, naming rivers and mountains and states or counties. Then draw a path on the map that demonstrates the most courageous route through this imaginary land. Compose a diary entry by a writer who explores that path.

## MOVING LINES

Nine at the beginning means that in order to lead, you must follow. To be a writer, then, means that you must follow the path of veteran writers before you can lead newer writers. Draw a map of the inside of your head, and show the path through it that your writerly self would take. Then write a short essay about what following that path means to you.

Six in the second place means you should choose your friends carefully. Choose only those friends who will help you find and follow the writer's path. Write a short essay in which you analyze what kind of friendship is most beneficial to the serious writer.

Six in the third place means you must discard friends who do not encourage you in your work as a writer. Choose as friends those people and books that show you how to be a writer. Write a short letter to a writer, living or dead, who you feel could help you in your work.

Nine in the fourth place means you should work hard at finding clarity — of vision, of purpose, of how to be in the world. Some friends are just followers who flatter you; you must follow the writer's path by being with people who, in contrast, are absolutely clear and free in their intentions. Write a short essay in which you describe what it is to walk in freedom and clarity.

Nine in the fifth place means that you will find good luck. Follow truth and beauty not just as ideals, but as people, events, or places you run across in your own life. Write a short essay in which you describe a truly beautiful person or place.

Six at the top means you will find a friend who already understands what it means to be a writer — and who will show you the way. This friend might be an editor, a companion, an author you meet by chance — someone you will recognize by his or her abilities. Write a short essay that describes the feeling of meeting someone who you know will grow very important to you.

## LAST WORD

When the right time arrives, you will be asked whether you prefer the writer's path to all other roads. Writers are people who write. Beware the choice you make when asked if you want a life as a writer. Perseverance along your chosen course is essential.

# 18. Ku

*Revise Your Work*

*With every question, before making any deep
examination of the content, I take a look at the language;
I generally proceed like a surgeon who sterilizes his hands
and prepares the area to be operated on.
This is what I call cleaning up the verbal situation.*

— PAUL VALÉRY

*Putting [the draft] aside for a couple of days is easiest and
best. The main point will often come perfectly clear to you
all by itself, as you are walking around doing something
entirely different or else when you sit down again after your
vacation. Your mind will chew on the problem by itself
while you are supposedly ignoring it. But if that doesn't
work, you'll just have to wrestle some more with that snake.*

— PETER ELBOW

## COMMENTARY

Throwing this hexagram means you must attend to the
revision of your work. Standard images of this hexagram
vary from a bowl filled with worms to a corroding pot. It is
the writer's job to set right that which has not been clear.

## PREDICTION

You will hunt for the right section to revise, and then rewrite that section beautifully.

## ADVISORY

Listen to your teachers, your friends, your writing partners, as you identify what to revise. But the actual work of revision must be yours. Use your inner ear as your guide. All revision is a normal part of the composing process.

## FOR THE WRITER

Read over the passage that you want to revise. Then turn your page over (or close the notebook) and start over from the beginning, writing out the whole passage from memory alone.

## MOVING LINES

Six at the beginning means there is some danger ahead. In the end, however, you will write and revise in a successful fashion. Take your work-in-progress and draw a squiggly line under all words, phrases, or passages that strike you as risky. Write out those words on a separate piece of paper, then evaluate as best you can whether they need revising. Revise those that do.

Nine in the second place means that you must be gentle with your revising. There is some risk in proceeding too abruptly or brusquely as you revise. Take your work-in-progress and draw a line in the margin next to any sentence or lyric that could be developed. Add some words, phrases, or paragraphs to the places you have marked.

Nine in the third place means you will have to revise those parts that you have already revised. That is, there will be parts of your writing that you have inadequately revised already. Start with a clean sheet of paper. Write down those sentences or passages that you plan to revise on that piece of paper. Start afresh, composing a better, fuller version of each passage.

Six in the fourth place means that humiliation is one possible outcome of this revising session. You must not only make cosmetic changes, but you must also get into the work more substantively. Locate a paragraph or a passage in your work that you really want to improve. Then rethink that passage for another audience, rewriting it completely to better address that new audience.

Six in the fifth place means that if you are thorough in your revisions, then you will meet with success. Writing a new beginning is the most beneficial prospect, but working with other people on any section of your writing is also good. Take a work-in-progress and try to write the beginning in a new and inventive way, with or without the help of friends.

Nine at the top means you are trying to write to a more sophisticated audience. Keep up the effort, but do not forget that you do so to educate and transform, not simply to entertain. Rewrite part of your work-in-progress so that it better addresses this new audience.

## LAST WORD

Learning your own process of revising takes hard work, both in identifying a passage and reworking that passage successfully. The main purposes of revising are (1) to make a piece of writing better, and (2) to teach yourself how to play with existing words. It is a process of fresh creation and continual practice in removing, adding, or shuffling words. All these activities — and concomitant thinking and feeling — are difficult and necessary.

# 19. LIN

*Overseeing the True Way*

*[Genius is] not a gift, but the way a person invents
in desperate circumstances.*

— JEAN-PAUL SARTRE

*Light breaks where no sun shines.*

— DYLAN THOMAS

## COMMENTARY

Writers often delude themselves, thinking that some lines
are extravagantly horrible or great. This hexagram indicates that if the writer perseveres in the true way, dispensing with all illusions, he or she will achieve great success.

## ADVISORY

The true way is very difficult to define. It is usually a way
of writing that listens to the heart, finds an authentic

voice, and perseveres no matter what the distraction. This hexagram suggests that you get rid of delusions and progress with diligence and care. Then success will come.

### PREDICTION

If you cut out all delusions and proceed as an honest, vulnerable writer, you will be very successful.

### FOR THE WRITER

Contemplate the inside of your own head. Do you see any dim spots, any red, any haze? These are the places where you are entertaining illusions about yourself. Clean away those places in your mind that stand in for your illusions, and write a paragraph about what it is like to have a mind that is like glass: clear, fresh, and free of illusion.

### MOVING LINES

Nine at the beginning means you should be cautious about your associations. Good is on the horizon, but only true friends can help you arrive there. Write a short essay about what it means to you to have a mind that is elegant and true.

Nine in the second place means everything you do will lead to good fortune. The future need not foster any concerns. Write a short essay in which you describe the future as a piece of glass.

Six in the third place means you should not relax

and think all is well. Remain vigilant, change your perspective as necessary, and you will find yourself back on the path to good fortune. Write a short poem in which you imagine your own life as a series of gates opening ahead of you. Where does each gate lead?

Six in the fourth place means that very favorable conditions are ahead. Remain open-minded and approachable to all people, and you will excel and succeed. Write a skit in which two people meet and become friends.

Six in the fifth place means you are very wise about choosing with whom to associate, how to spend your money, and where people around you need light guidance or a heavy hand. Wisdom and success follow all your actions. Write a page or two about whatever you wish.

Six at the top means you will enjoy great success in your writing. You will help other people with their work, and by doing so help yourself immensely. All is good, in life and in work. Write two pages wherein you open one of two gates. Behind one, you will find a large and beautiful piece of blue glass; behind the other, you will find a gorgeous piece of gneiss, as large and as fulgent as the stone that marks Ralph Waldo Emerson's grave. What would each mean in your life as a writer? Which gate would you choose?

### LAST WORD

If you are faithful to the true way — the one path that is absolutely right for you — you will achieve great success.

# 20. Kuan

*Observe*

*If a writer stops observing, he is finished.*

— ERNEST HEMINGWAY

*[O]ne has the urge, first of all, to order the facts
one observes and to give meaning to life;
and along with that goes the love of words for their
own sake and a desire to manipulate them.*

— ALDOUS HUXLEY

## COMMENTARY

The ability to cut off delusions requires absolutely accurate observations. If you look around you right now, for example, you might observe some aspect of your surroundings that you have never before noticed. Ironically, when a writer erases all delusions that obscure her true vision, she herself will be seen more clearly.

## PREDICTION

You will learn how to look without looking, to see without seeing, to touch without touching. You will learn some truths about the world, and your expression of those truths will be utterly sincere.

## ADVISORY

Take a moment to observe the space in which you compose. What do you see, hear, smell, feel? How do you imagine the surroundings would taste? How does the quality of your mind change according to these observations? To observe well, without veil or delusion, is to see the world within the world.

## FOR THE WRITER

Find a pet, bug, bird, or any animal to observe. Write down ten adjectives that describe that creature. Write down ten verbs that describe that creature's movements. Then write a narrative poem (see Glossary, p. 280) describing five minutes in that creature's life.

## MOVING LINES

Six at the beginning means you need to practice contemplation. Contemplation is both an internal and an external exercise: let the world enter you and you enter the world. Stare at a spot about six feet from you for several minutes. Then write a page on what happens to you when you slow yourself down and simply watch the world.

Six in the second place means that observation will be difficult. It will be like trying to see through the crack of a door. Consider your own hands. What were they doing before you began writing today? What will they do after you are through writing? Write a page in free verse (see Glossary, p. 278), in which you describe your hands as though they belonged to someone else.

Six in the third place means that you will make a transition from egoism to real self-knowledge. You are learning the hard lesson that to observe yourself means to examine the meaning of your life, to gauge whether the effects of your life are positive or negative. Write a narrative poem (see Glossary, p. 280) in which you analyze what it means to have lived a good life.

Six in the fourth place means that your observations lead to influence. You understand secrets. Write a page or two in which you describe at least two photographs in an imaginary exhibit of other people's secrets.

Nine in the fifth place means that you know how to contemplate your own life. You have good perspective and inner vision. Write a page or two, in prose or poetry, in which you reflect on the meaning of your life.

Nine at the top means you have successfully tamed your own ego. You are like a sage who stands outside the world and contemplates the meaning of life from that viewpoint. Write a manifesto in which each sentence begins with some form of the statement, "I believe..."

## LAST WORD

If you observe without placing yourself in the middle of that observation, you will catch glimpses of the actual reality of which we are all a part. There is no more important work than looking out at the world and learning how to see, without ourselves in the picture.

# 21. Shih Ho

*Persevere in Your Work*

*Schiller liked to have a smell of rotten apples, concealed beneath the lid of his desk, under his nose when he was composing poetry. Walter de la Mare has told me he must smoke when writing. Auden drinks endless cups of tea. Coffee is my own addiction, besides smoking a great deal, which I hardly ever do except when I am writing.*

— STEPHEN SPENDER

*I suppose really focused writing takes a year. But sometimes a book takes ages. It refuses to gel. That is why in spite of computers and the Internet and working hard — all of which should make you very productive — writing is always very difficult. Always.*

— PAT BARKER

## COMMENTARY

There come times when all one can do is persevere. This is one of those times. Persevere in your work, bite through opposition and obstacles, and eventually success will come. Beware the people who slow you down as you try to continue the work. Beware the gossip, the glutton, the slothful, the flatterer, the liar. Any or all of these may stand between you and the successful completion of your work.

## PREDICTION

You will achieve success in your writing, but it will only come after a long period of endurance and perseverance.

## ADVISORY

Sometimes it is going to feel as though you are making no progress in your work. In fact, you are making great progress, but it is slow. Keep your head down, avoid the detractors, and keep inching forward. Your work is bound to be a great success.

## FOR THE WRITER

Write down all the negative experiences you have ever had with writing.

## MOVING LINES

Nine at the beginning means you must stop immediately and evaluate your work-in-progress. There is something you are doing that can lead to real trouble in your writing process. Free write (see Glossary, p. 278) about any problems you are having now with your writing. Pause, then circle the one that seems most relevant now. Think about how to solve it.

Six in the second place means that everything will

turn out all right. However, there is a tendency to lose discrimination and sensitivity. Write down five true (and encouraging) things you know about writing, then post that list where you can see it.

Six in the third place means that someone else is going to judge your work and make suggestions. Ignore that person, whose motives are not pure and who lacks the background to make such judgments. Write a list of every characteristic you would expect of your ideal reader.

Nine in the fourth place means there will be difficulties, but you still must persevere. There is good luck ahead. Write a page or two about what it means to you to persevere in your writing career.

Six in the fifth place means that the way ahead will not be easy, but what to do will be clear. In the midst of pressures to be overly responsible or irresponsible in your writing, you must strive to embrace the middle way. Write a page or two about what it means to you to take the middle way in your writing process.

Nine at the top means you will experience misfortune with your writing in the near term. However, you will avoid real misfortune if you listen to the warnings coming your way from others. Write a series of ten sentences, each of which begins, "When I write, I know..."

## LAST WORD

Enduring as a writer is a tough prospect, but it is absolutely necessary, especially at this time. Persevere in developing your work, honing your writing process, and finding true purpose in what you write, and you will achieve success.

# 22. PI

*Put in the Delicate Touches*

*I don't believe in the importance of scale; to me the moralist is no more valid than the miniature painter. In this very large country, where size is all... I am content to stitch away at my embroidery hoop. I think the form I work can have its own distinction.*

— S. J. PERELMAN

*It's like when you realize that a couple of notes make a melody or song. There's no exact moment, but you have something over here, and then placing it in counterpoint makes a sound. You go, Hmm, this is something.*

— KEVIN YOUNG

## COMMENTARY

Choosing this hexagram signifies the importance of working on the smaller pieces of the writing process. It suggests that paying attention to the sentence or line is most crucial; to attend to the ornament rather than the structure is essential. Such attention brings success to the writer.

## PREDICTION

If you work hard at putting in the delicate touches, you will achieve real grace and beauty in your work.

## ADVISORY

This hexagram is best selected toward the end of the writing process because that is the proper time to attend to light editing. If you throw this hexagram very early in your composing, its advice probably applies more to your conception of the piece than to the sentence-level editing it normally would suggest. If it is early in the writing process, think in subtle, nuanced ways about how to present your topic or frame your content.

## FOR THE WRITER

Put on a soft, unobtrusive piece of music and write to it. Choose a page to work on. Revise by removing all adjectives and adverbs. Then make the verbs more powerful. (Instead of saying, for example, "He ran quickly across the room," say, "He galloped across the room.")

## MOVING LINES

Nine at the beginning means you are at the start of an important phase of your writing project. It is best that you approach this phase without pretension or arrogance. Take it slowly. Turn on some quiet music, then write a letter to yourself about how you want to proceed in the next phase of your project.

Six in the second place means you should be concentrating more on content than form as you write and revise your work. Form will follow later. Turn on some quiet music and write a letter to a friend explaining what the primary content, message, and purpose of your current project might be.

Nine in the third place means success is at hand, as long as you do not sink into complacency. Beware the indolence and lethargy that come with great success. Persevere in your writing. Write a page or two of reminders to yourself about what you intend to do in this next phase of the writing process.

Six in the fourth place means that you will have to choose between great beauty and great simplicity in your work. Both are a matter of personal style. Which shall you choose? This moving line suggests that simplicity is the better choice for you. Write two short essays, one defining simplicity and the other defining beauty.

Six in the fifth place means that sincere writing is worth more than all the gold in the world. Do not be ashamed of your material status; know that your words, especially simple words, are valuable. Write a prose poem (see Glossary, p. 281) in which you use no word of more than one syllable. Have beauty be your subject.

Nine at the top means you will find success through simple grace. Form and content are perfectly wed. Write a paragraph for the beginning of an essay about building (or making) something beautiful.

## LAST WORD

You will find good fortune when you apply light pressure to your own writing. Put in the delicate touches only. Be sincere and simple in your writing, revise accordingly, and your writing will be successful.

# 23. Po

*Strip Away Illusion*

*I think every creative impulse that a working writer,
or artist of any sort, has comes out of that
dark old country where dreams come from.*

— ANNE RIVERS SIDDONS

*In fact, every creation, every vision of life, every
revelation of the spirit, necessarily carries within itself
problems, questions, logical contradictions... and this
simply because mystery is congenital to the spirit,
and to look with new eyes, to express frankly, to
reorganize life is to project life once more in mystery.*

— LUIGI PIRANDELLO

## COMMENTARY

While it is true that all genuine writing springs from
the heart, arises from that welter that is dream and sigh
combined, it is important to look at your writing in the
cold light of day. It is not to your benefit to start any
new project until you have undertaken such examination. Separate your vision and your illusions, and your
writing will radiate its new purity.

## PREDICTION

Unless you separate illusion from truth, both in your writing and in your life, you will suffer.

## ADVISORY

Stop writing for a little while and consider how you are fooling yourself. What is the real intent of your writing? Who is really benefiting from your supposed charitable relationships? Examine your own motives and desires with cold-hearted realism; what you find may surprise you.

## FOR THE WRITER

Write about some secret that you are keeping from yourself — and everyone else.

## MOVING LINES

Six at the beginning bodes ill. Disaster awaits. Write a flash fiction (see Glossary, p. 278) about a dishonest coworker.

Six in the second place means you are in a very dangerous situation. No help is coming. Write a flash fiction (see Glossary, p. 278) in which someone reveals a secret to you that is entirely unexpected.

Six in the third place means you are at great risk but help is on its way. You will see the truth in your own writing and strip away illusion; then all will be right.

Write a flash fiction (see Glossary, p. 278) in which a man buys a dog who isn't at all what he expected her to be.

Six in the fourth place means grave misfortune. Do not rest. Write a flash fiction (see Glossary, p. 278) in which a young woman reveals her darkest secret and is rejected because of it.

Six in the fifth place means you will find salvation from danger through turning away from illusion. A strong person will join you in turning toward the light. Write a short essay in which you define the word "secret" and talk about what compels us to keep secrets.

Nine at the top means that times are improving. The work is getting easier because the illusions you hold to are dissipating. Write a poem about a person who tells all the secrets he or she has; show us the consequences.

## LAST WORD

Pay special attention from this day forward to the ways in which you fool yourself and build insincerity into your writing. Be true and honest in everything you say. Split apart illusion from truth, and you will enter a new world.

# 24. Fu

## *Return to the Work (Turning Around)*

*Come back to your writing with enthusiasm
and generosity. You are not reacquainting yourself
with an old friend but making a new one.*

— JUDY DOENGES

*[My teacher] always said that if your writing is good,
it will find a home without a lot of hustling and scheming.
And he was right — once my writing was ready,
things had a way of falling into place.*

— MARY YUKARI WATERS

### COMMENTARY

After a period of frustration and delay, this is the turning point. If you return to your work with the right attitude and energy, you will enjoy success. Working on the ending will be particularly profitable. But it is important not to force yourself; take it slow and easy, finding your own pace. Then your work will be profitable. The time of the winter solstice may be particularly important.

## PREDICTION

You will find your way to your writing again and enjoy success. It may take as long as a week to regain your momentum, but the turning point will come and you will enjoy your writing again.

## ADVISORY

All writing moves in a kind of cycle, from easy to frustrating, from satisfying to disappointing, from heavenly feelings of accomplishment to earthly feelings of being inept. Recognize that you are on the upswing here, and with just a little attention you will find yourself enjoying success. Take it slowly, but you may be confident of the final outcome.

## FOR THE WRITER

Choose a page to return to. When you return, pay attention to the music of the language; observe the meter and cadence (see Glossary, pp. 280 and 277). Experiment with different rhythms. Rewrite your page as a fairy tale.

## MOVING LINES

Nine at the beginning means that there will be great fortune. Practice leads to a great success. Choose a page to return to and revise it according to its rhythms. Rewrite the page as a myth of someone who becomes successful after great effort.

Six in the second place means that the return to

your work will be quiet and easy. No need to hurry; you will find success at any rate. Just for fun, rewrite your work in the form of a fairy tale.

Six in the third place means that you will return to your work several times. There is some danger that the work will not progress as you wished. Revise a page that is incomplete. Add sentences or lines that make it more musical, that accentuate your meaning. Then rewrite the page in the form of an urban legend (see Glossary, p. 282).

Six in the fourth place means that your progress through the revising process will be done alone. While other people may be around, only you will go in and do the hard work; the outcome will be good. Play with meter (see Glossary, p. 280) in a page of your writing; try iambic pentameter (see Glossary, p. 279) in a sentence, for example. Rewrite your page in the form of a legend.

Six in the fifth place means there will be no time for evasions or cosmetic revisions. Further, if you have done something seriously wrong, either in your writing or in a relationship with another writer, own up to it and ask for forgiveness. Revise a page in which you add a musical detail — for example, add a song playing in the background while two people chat, a sheet of music on the floor, a piano in the corner, something.

Six at the top means that you will miss the opportunity to return to the work unless you concentrate very hard. There is real danger of bad fortune here, caused primarily by your stubbornness in holding to a wrong attitude. Think through your revision strategy and change it. Revise a page of your work-in-progress, trying something brand-new in your approach, perhaps re-writing it as a romance.

## LAST WORD

Changing an attitude, returning to a work-in-progress when one has been discouraged, is surely difficult. However, that is what this hexagram calls for. You must not only revise your work, but you must revise yourself as well. Nothing is harder than self-transformation, which must start with self-awareness. Slow down and ask yourself what needs to change in your encounters with your writing, in your relationships with other people. Overall, this hexagram indicates that such self-examination and transformation will be successful.

# 25. WU WANG

*Write Spontaneously*

*The unconscious is the ocean of the unsayable, of what has been expelled from the land of language, removed as a result of ancient prohibitions. The unconscious speaks — in dreams, in verbal slips, in sudden associations — with borrowed words, stolen symbols, linguistic contraband, until literature redeems these territories and annexes them to the language of the waking world.*

— ITALO CALVINO

*What I really do is take real plums and put them in an imaginary cake.*

— MARY MCCARTHY

## COMMENTARY

This hexagram indicates that your deepest self is true. When you proceed with innocence, without ulterior motive or secret agenda, you will achieve success in your writing. You must write spontaneously, without guile, noting the unexpected and evanescent insight, being true to that which needs expression right now.

## PREDICTION

Discover your own innocence, and you will write a beautiful first draft.

## ADVISORY

Usually this hexagram indicates that you must pull out a sheet of paper and write blindly, quickly, from the depths of your heart. Fake nothing. Tell the truth as you know it. Do not lose your innocence.

## FOR THE WRITER

Write as quickly as you can any lines that might look and sound like nonsense. Fill up a page. Then circle words or phrases that you like. Start again with three of those words or phrases and write nonsense about them. Free yourself of the usual conventions of writing. Be as silly as you wish.

## MOVING LINES

Nine at the beginning means that if we write from the heart, spontaneously, the outcome will be a good one. The true impulses of the heart are always good; it is just hearing them that is sometimes hard. Take out a sheet of paper and quickly write everything you hear your own heart saying. Then, if you have time, take out another sheet of paper and respond. Have a conversation with your own heart.

Six in the second place means that we should undertake each writing task as it is demanded of us, right now. We should not anticipate the overall outcome or think about why we are doing this writing and revision. Write a letter to a close friend in which you tell him or her how you are feeling right now. Be honest.

Six in the third place means that you are going to hit a snag in your attempts to write spontaneously. And that misfortune is out of your hands; there is nothing you can do. Write a short poem in which you lament the lost opportunity to simply compose from the heart, without interruption.

Nine in the fourth place means that you cannot lose your direction or heart even if you try to throw it away. What we are meant to do or be is always clear to us. Write the first draft of a letter to yourself in which you apologize for throwing away some part of yourself.

Nine in the fifth place means that you will be beset by an accident or illness that is not your fault. Pay no attention and do not seek external aids; all you need to heal is right here. Write a free-verse poem (see Glossary, p. 278) about an accident either you or a friend has had.

Nine at the top means you should not act if the moment is not right. Proceed quietly, picking the moment when you should respond spontaneously and wonderingly about the world. Revise a page of writing that seems to need it right now.

## LAST WORD

To write spontaneously is to acknowledge the truths that lodge inside. The truths are already there, waiting for their turn at the door. Just listen to your heart and trust its instincts. If more people followed their heart's soft music, we would have a more compassionate, authentic world.

# 26. TA CH'U

## *Hold Firm to Art's Exquisite Path*

*Art is a vocation, as much as anything in this world. For
the real artist, it is the most natural thing in the world,
not as necessary as air and water, perhaps, but as food and
water. But we really do lead almost a monastic life,
you know; to follow it you very often have to give up
something.... Courage is the first essential.*

— KATHERINE ANNE PORTER

*[Art] is allied with the good and its foundation is goodness,
closely akin to wisdom, even more closely to love.*

— THOMAS MANN

### COMMENTARY

This hexagram shows you overcoming the small irrita-
tions and minor problems that beset any writer. You
proceed along art's exquisite path, knowing that other
writers have passed this way before you. A long journey,
perhaps over water, beckons to you. This hexagram shows
you not hesitating as you continue on your chosen path.

## PREDICTION

You will hold fast to your dreams and stay steady on this exquisite path.

## ADVISORY

Stay the course. You must balance your creativity as a writer with a firm commitment to learning — and doing — more with your craft. The way ahead is clear if you stay committed to daily attention to your writing, and to your own character. Success will be at hand if you pursue these tasks.

## FOR THE WRITER

Write down all your successes as a writer. Which ones are most important to you? What do they show about you as a writer?

## MOVING LINES

Nine at the beginning means there is a real risk to your career as a writer. Stay where you are and stay calm; to move ahead now is to risk real misfortune. Write a page about one of the times when you feel you got unfair comments or cruel responses to your writing.

    Nine in the second place means that you should stay where you are and wait for the right moment to release all your creative energy. Every moment that you wait, your strength grows. Write a note to yourself about what changes you will make to your writing habits when the time is ripe.

    Nine in the third place means that the way is now

clear. However, there is still danger in the journey along art's exquisite path; heed the need for caution. Write a page in which you detail for yourself the next step in your current writing project.

Six in the fourth place means that very good luck lies ahead. You will persevere on your path, and no obstacle shall block your journey. Write a list of tricks you have discovered for writing well. Write the list so that you will remember some of the tricks later, when you need them most.

Six in the fifth place also means that good luck lies ahead. You should not use force to proceed along the path, but let your own nature show you what to do. For ten minutes, write whatever comes into your head. Circle those parts that strike you as significant, and write some more about them.

Nine at the top means you will achieve success. The way to heaven is along art's exquisite path, and you have proceeded past all obstacles to arrive there. Write a page or two in which you talk about your own character as you proceed down the last leg of the journey along art's exquisite path.

## LAST WORD

With or without obstacles, following art's exquisite path is a difficult enterprise. It requires strength of character as well as strength as a writer. As you proceed in your writing career, show courage even in the darkest times. You will eventually find your way if you continue down art's winding path.

# 27. I

*Nourish the Life of a Writer*

*We can in the end prevail, if our attachment
to art is sufficiently deep; unpriggish, subtle,
perceptive, and consuming.*

— MARIANNE MOORE

*Part of the action is to keep taking in. Use everything.*

— C. D. WRIGHT

## COMMENTARY

To know what kind of writer a person is, observe his habits. What does the writer do to nurture the composing process? When and where does he write? Does she write every day? The character of a writer is easily revealed by watching her. This hexagram encourages you to take very good care of your writerly self; nourish your writing through your own habits, conversation, and preparation. Show daily concern for your writing.

## PREDICTION

You will learn to be careful with your words and not use them loosely or without thought. You will learn how to nourish yourself and develop the habits of a serious writer.

## ADVISORY

Be wary of comparing yourself too much with other writers. Your primary task is to nurture yourself as a writer. Look to your own habits and rituals of writing; make sure they promote your talent and health. Let other concerns go.

## FOR THE WRITER

Write a list of at least ten sentences, each of which begins: "A writer is someone who..."

## MOVING LINES

Nine at the beginning means that your search for nourishment as a writer will initially fail. Beware of comparing yourself to others and becoming envious. Write ten sentences, each one beginning with "I am a writer who is able to..."

Six in the second place means that misfortune may occur if you do not learn how to nurture yourself. Too much reliance on others hurts your own abilities to be independent and free. Write a list of ten things that nourish you as a writer.

Six in the third place means that you are seeking to nourish yourself through gratification of sensual desire alone. With moderation, satisfying sensual desire is an excellent way to proceed. However, in excess it leaves the writer unhappy and empty. Write a flash fiction (see Glossary, p. 278) in which two people "fall in lust."

Six in the fourth place means good fortune. You are working for the good of other people as well as yourself. Write a short free-verse poem (see Glossary, p. 278) in which you talk about the influence of other writers (famous or not) on you.

Six in the fifth place means to seek the help of an older, more successful person. Follow that person's lead, avoid confrontation with others, and it will benefit you as a writer. Write a short character sketch (see Glossary, p. 277) of someone you know who is older and successful.

Nine at the top means that, thanks to the advice of a stranger, you are aware of danger to yourself. By being aware, you are able to sidestep the danger and arrive at good fortune. Write the first page of a fairy tale in which the protagonist (see Glossary, p. 281) is preparing to fight some danger far ahead.

## LAST WORD

Nourishing yourself as a writer is important to your developing talent and ultimate success. Be very good to yourself. Develop the habits and set of mind that serious writers, by and large, maintain. Do not be distracted by the exotic or intoxicating, except in moderation. Seek those experiences that are of substance, that fill you with hope and meaning.

# 28. Ta Kuo

## Crisis in Writing

*After the awful beginning come the months of freewheeling play, and after the play come the crises, turning against your material and hating the book.*

— PHILIP ROTH

*Even when I sit at my typewriter, I feel as if what I wrote were written by an imbecile ten miles off.*

— SYLVIA PLATH

## COMMENTARY

This hexagram reveals that there is something wrong with your work-in-progress. It is as though you have built a house using beams that are too thin at the ends and very thick in the middle. Danger. Risk. Take great care as you revise; it is extraordinarily important that you do it well.

## PREDICTION

Your work-in-progress will collapse unless you pay close attention. If you revise those parts that are flawed or incomplete, success may still occur.

### ADVISORY

Proceed with great caution as you build and dismantle parts of your work-in-progress. There are grave dangers here, but also possibility for success. It all depends on your abilities to discern where to change what you have written. Be careful and rely on your best instincts.

### FOR THE WRITER

Write about a problem with your writing right now. Write about how it evolved and how you expect it to evolve further; compare it to other kinds of problems you've had with writing. Propose a solution.

### MOVING LINES

Six at the beginning means you need to exercise extraordinary caution as you continue to write this piece. Caution must especially be taken in laying the foundation of the work-in-progress; the first draft, the shape of the piece, or how it actually begins should be your focus. Write a short memo to yourself about the structure of your work-in-progress.

Nine in the second place means that you should listen to advice, no matter how unlikely the quarter from which it comes. If you have some writing you attempted in the past, return to it now. Write a revision of a poem or prose piece that you wrote a long time ago.

Nine in the third place means bad luck is ahead, in part because you will not listen to the advice of others. Do not plunge ahead in your writing process without acknowledging the danger of moving too fast; take it slowly. Write a poem in which the first letter of each line spells a word vertically, such as your own name or the name of someone you care about.

Nine in the fourth place means that there is danger of humiliating yourself by running after powerful others. Keep in mind how people less able than you can still help you. Write a short letter to someone in your writing group or someone else who is trying to write, explaining your difficulties.

Nine in the fifth place means that nothing changes, to the point of all being barren. When you are revising, it is important to listen to all advice and to change your words according to what makes the most sense, not according to the importance of the person who said it. Write a poem about an older woman who takes a husband but is unable to have children anymore.

Six at the top means you may have to save your writing at the cost of giving up something else. You can't do it all and survive. Write a prose poem (see Glossary, p. 281) about what it means to choose between one's writing and something else that's important.

## LAST WORD

This hexagram is probably the most dangerous one to throw. It forces hard choices; it demands fair and democratic behavior; it asks writers to choose between their craft and their family, friends, or other important work. If you throw this hexagram, you must proceed with grave caution. However, if you make good decisions, success will still be yours. It just might not come in the way you expected it.

# 29. K'AN

*Danger in Writing*

*I looked in the arsenal and found another dynamite stick,
and I thought, "Light the fuse and see what happens."
I was trying to blow up more of myself.
This phenomenon is known to students of literary
survey courses as the writer changing his style.*

— PHILIP ROTH

*We suffer from the use of language to conceal thought and
to withhold all vital and direct answers.*

— EZRA POUND

## COMMENTARY

This hexagram connotes the power of human beings to
overcome danger, if only they will behave like a stream
pouring down a canyon. That is, water will always seek
its own edge, will pour to the bottom of the ravine quite
naturally. People must learn to be as natural, supple, and
encompassing. Then danger will pass or be mastered.

## PREDICTION

Danger passes if the writer relies upon her natural abilities and wit.

## ADVISORY

You may find the abyss underlying your writing. You may sense the danger that is inherent in composing in any form. Work on your personal character, and your writing (and other art) will improve. You should develop goodness and compassion as an antidote to danger. Have goodness and compassion become permanent parts of your character, rather than the result of accident.

## FOR THE WRITER

Write about the most dangerous part of your writing process. Imagine it as a hungry, angry animal. Describe that fierce animal, then explain how you will cope with it.

## MOVING LINES

Six at the beginning means that you have lost your way. You are growing used to evil, and must resist it more strongly. Write a brief manifesto (a statement of belief) in which you explain what it means to have good character.

Nine in the second place means your writing process is still in danger. If you revise today, revise only lightly. Look at your work-in-progress and play with the sentences, single words, punctuation — but do not attempt any whole-cloth revisions today.

Six in the third place means you are still in danger as a writer, and there is no escape from that danger. Therefore, do not act rashly; stay still. Write a series of ten sentences that all begin, "To be in real danger means..."

Six in the fourth place means that your sincerity as a writer matters more than anything right now. Someone near you is going to need help, and as you offer it recognize that the help will be mutual in the near future. Write a short essay in which you talk about how to cope with sickness.

Nine in the fifth place means that you are too ambitious and don't recognize the intensive labor required of writers. Take your time, progress more slowly, and recognize that success comes only after hard work. Write a memorandum telling yourself how to cope with your own ambitions.

Six at the top means that there is no escape from your flaws and problems as a writer — unless you recognize them and painstakingly strive to correct them, one by one. Write a flash fiction (see Glossary, p. 278) featuring a man at the bottom of a pit, trying to get help to get out.

## LAST WORD

Writing is always a dangerous art. Words have real power, and words arranged in particular constellations have even more power. Beware the dangers of words even as you embrace them. You write from the point of gravest danger; such a location cannot be better for authenticity, sincerity, and genuine speech. Cope well with the dangers, and you will be an even better writer than you already are.

# 30. LI

## *Enlightenment*

*[Fiction] doesn't have to do anything. It just has to be there for the fierce pleasure we take in doing it, and the different kind of pleasure that's taken in reading something that's durable and made to last, as well as beautiful in and of itself. Something that throws off these sparks — a persistent and steady glow, however dim.*

— RAYMOND CARVER

*It is not within me that the true unity of my work comes about. I have written a "score" — but I can hear it only when performed by the soul and the mind of someone else.*

— PAUL VALÉRY

## COMMENTARY

Enlightenment is a kind of fire that arrives after meditation, self-analysis, the slow gathering of knowledge of one's own character. The fire burns away the conditioning we all have. Feeding this fire requires a certain frame of mind — and training that allows our mind to become flexible and truly aware of this reality. This hexagram shows fire above and fire below — trigrams that indicate a double benefit, a tandem ignition of enlightenment.

## PREDICTION

If you continue practicing the way of a writer, you will find the fire.

## ADVISORY

Take your work as a writer quite seriously because it will ultimately lead to an enlightenment beyond words. Regularity in your writing habits will help foster this enlightenment, especially regularity in the time of day when you write. Developing a knowledge of your own nature, as a writer and as a person, will help you develop the character you need to contribute wisely to the larger community.

## FOR THE WRITER

Write about a secret you know about somebody else.

## MOVING LINES

Nine at the beginning means pay attention to your habits early in the morning. It is essential that you start each day, or each period of writing, with a clear head and a calm mind. Write a page in which you explore the secret life of someone with whom you work or live.

Six in the second place is very auspicious. You will achieve your greatest dreams for your writing and other arts. Write a page in which you reveal your own secret desires.

Nine in the third place is less auspicious. You will lose freedom, energy, and good attitude if you persevere on this path. Write a page in which you reveal a secret of someone older than you.

Nine in the fourth place means that you are at risk of burning fast, of rising and falling like a meteor. Do not let your highly excitable nature overcome your good sense and lead you astray. Write a page in which you talk about the secrets of the stars.

Six in the fifth place means good fortune. You understand better the pride of the self and the vanity of all creatures, and you adjust your good intentions accordingly. Write a page in which you tell the secret of someone you know who is quite vain.

Nine at the top means you must root out all bad habits in yourself to achieve enlightenment. Don't worry about the habits that bring no harm; simply work hard to end those habits that hurt others or yourself. Write a page in which you tell the secrets of your hands.

## LAST WORD

Enlightenment is a well-worn term, one that many traditions name as their ideal. In your case, enlightenment will come when you find your writing process in step with your character and mind. Take care in writing, because doing it well will lead to the fire of knowing.

# 31. Hsien

*Find a Writing Partner*

*When a collaboration works, the two people
concerned become a third person, who is different
from either of them in isolation.*

— W. H. AUDEN

*[N]othing is so powerful as a chance to see your words
through the eyes of others.*

— PETER ELBOW

## COMMENTARY

This hexagram is represented as a lake on top of a
mountain, lake and mountain connecting together like
two people engaged in the same enterprise. It is also
represented as two people uniting, the youngest son
marrying the youngest daughter. The hexagram signifies the importance of finding a valuable partner, someone who will connect closely to your intentions in your
writing and offer sound advice.

## PREDICTION

You will find a writing partner quite easily, and the two of you will work together for a long while.

## ADVISORY

Pick your writing partner carefully. He or she should be someone you instinctively like, who is considerate and enlivens you, and who shares your aesthetic and your goals. Beware the writing partner who is glib, cavalier, or unreliable. Choose carefully.

## FOR THE WRITER

Write a portrait of someone you love.

## MOVING LINES

Six at the beginning means there is little movement and little influence. Your intention to find a writing partner is developing, but you have done little to actually nurture such a new relationship. Write a page in which you describe falling in love with a writing partner.

Six in the second place means there is movement, but movement toward misfortune. Stop and wait until the person who will make the best writing partner for you is more clearly revealed. Write a page in which you describe two people who love each other very much but never actually touch each other.

Nine in the third place means there may be some humiliation ahead. Do not let your feelings gallop ahead, but choose carefully *who* to ask to be your writing partner and *when* to do the asking. Proceed cautiously. Write a page in which you describe someone older than you and slightly unpleasant.

Nine in the fourth place means that good fortune shall attend your selection of a writing partner. Your heart will guide you, and you will find a very good person with whom to share your writing. Write a page in which you describe the inside of a heart in love.

Nine in the fifth place means that your unconscious and conscious minds are working together to select the best possible partner for you. There is no undue influence and no remorse; take your time, and the best person will occur to you. Write a page in which you describe the feeling at the back of your neck when someone you love walks by.

Six at the top means that you will try to persuade someone to be your writing partner. You will talk too much, and too superficially, in your attempts to persuade someone to join the enterprise. Write a letter to someone you love. Give it to him or her when you are done.

### LAST WORD

Once you have chosen a writing partner, enjoy him or her and learn as much as you can from that person. But also pay attention to the fit between you and your peer. Do you work well together? Is there laughter as well as long slogs through revisions? Find someone you enjoy who can help you.

# 32. HÊNG

*Endurance*

*After years of working crap jobs and raising kids*
*and trying to write, I realized I needed to write things*
*I could finish and be done with in a hurry...*
*Hence, poems and stories.*

— RAYMOND CARVER

*Writing is so hard.*
*It's the only time in your life when you have to think.*

— ELIZABETH HARDWICK

## COMMENTARY

In this hexagram, thunder above springs from wind below. Perseverance is required if lightning and its dangers are to be averted. This hexagram indicates the importance of endurance in the ever-shifting partnership of writer and writing. Seasons, days, planets, and moon all have their own rhythms. You must develop similar habits of regularity, endurance, a familiar beauty returning. Endure because it keeps you safer and allows your work to ferment in beneficial fashion.

## PREDICTION

If you follow the inner laws of your being, what you write will endure for generations.

## ADVISORY

Do not try to force writing out of yourself if the time is not ripe or the effort not sincere. Thunder and wind are signs of impermanence, but the permanence of their nature is the same as yours: recurring patterns become enduring cycles. Be aware of your own patterns of behavior, patterns of writing. Nurture those patterns even as you acknowledge the impermanence of rituals and works.

## FOR THE WRITER

What does *sanctuary* look like to you? Is it in the woods? Does it have a religious aspect? Is it part of a community, or is it solitary? Is it a cave or a tree house or some other dwelling? Write two pages about a sanctuary that would nourish you.

## MOVING LINES

Six at the beginning means that if you seek to endure when the work itself is unbalanced, misfortune will follow. Long work and careful reflection are required to balance a work of writing. Write two pages in which you imagine your perfect sanctuary — a place that is peaceful, stable, and enduring.

Nine in the second place means that your ambition may sometimes outweigh your experience in writing. Do not attempt something that is beyond your experience or knowledge at this time. Write two pages in which you describe the sanctuary to which you would retreat to gain a clearer perspective on the work ahead.

Nine in the third place means you may face humiliation sometime in the near future. Your nature may be obscured by flights of fancy, inconsistent acts, or insufficient self-knowledge. Know thyself. Write two pages in which you describe a sanctuary designed primarily to keep you grounded, prepared for work, peaceful, and sane.

Nine in the fourth place means you will not easily find a way to endure. Even worse, persistence is not enough. Change your definition of endurance and your strategy for enduring. Write two pages in which you describe a sanctuary that will crumble to dust in a day.

Six in the fifth place means good fortune for a woman, bad fortune for a man. In either case, try to identify your commitment to your writing and develop it. Write two pages in which you describe a sanctuary that nurtures both men and women.

Six at the top means that you have an abiding restlessness that must be tamed. You are living in a state of constant hurrying, which is of danger both to yourself and others. Write two pages in which you imagine a sanctuary that is designed to slow you down.

## LAST WORD

"Endurance" is the watchword of strict disciplinarians as well as those who are sick or wounded. We are all the walking wounded in some way. This hexagram reminds you to take care of yourself as you walk through this impermanent world, sigh through the sometimes interminable season of being.

# 33. Tun

*Turn Away from Those Who Would*
*Weaken Your Writing Practice*

*I may also be unusually resistant to what others tell me*
*to do — a condition that describes many writers,*
*and also a number of psychopaths.*

— ANN BEATTIE

*Necessity and struggle, based on a severe love, temper the*
*artist's soul, which becomes soft and decayed by easy flattery.*

— FEDERICO GARCÍA LORCA

## COMMENTARY

There is little cause for celebration in this hexagram. It is necessary to retreat from an encroaching darkness, to seek out those friends who will hold you up during this trying time. Avoid those who would hurt or misdirect you. This hexagram usually operates from July to August, or at the moment when the summer starts brooding about winter's arrival months away. There is a meaning hidden in such a trying time.

## PREDICTION

Someone you know casually will seek to grow closer, and if you respond you will find your energy rapidly diminishing.

## ADVISORY

Beware the new friend, or even the old one, who is suddenly working hard to distract you from your writing practice. Stand firm in your efforts to observe a schedule and a steady practice. Politely step away from those who would weaken you.

## FOR THE WRITER

Remember an acquaintance — a friend or an enemy — who persistently drains you of energy. It might be a needy friend, the acquaintance who always complains, the coworker who passes along poisonous gossip. First, write out an example of that person being up to his or her tricks. Second, write a short scene in which you encounter that person and tell him (or her) the truth about himself. Then walk away.

## MOVING LINES

Six at the beginning means that you must rapidly retreat from people who are not real friends. You are in danger and must not start a new project. Write a short essay in which you describe the dangers of false friends.

Six in the second place means that you should make haste to follow writers who are more experienced than you. Stay very close to those writers, and you will survive the danger you are currently in. Write a short essay in which you describe what it means to walk away from a false friend.

Nine in the third place means that some friends in your life are unpleasant. Danger still persists. Write a short essay in which you write a character sketch (see Glossary, p. 277) of an unpleasant friend, either real or imagined.

Nine in the fourth place means you should be at your best in character, ability, and intention. Only then will you survive and thrive despite the danger you are in. Write a short essay in which you describe yourself in your best aspect.

Nine in the fifth place means that the friends who weaken your practice are neither unkind nor ill-intentioned. They are true friends who just sometimes get in the way. Write a short essay about your favorite friend.

Nine at the top means that you are quite cheerful as you rearrange your writing life to accommodate your friends and your own promises to yourself. Stay true to your writing, but also make room for those who genuinely love you. Write a short essay in which you advise readers about balancing their writing life with their love life.

## LAST WORD

Avoid the darkness today, and step closer to the light. Retreat if necessary from those seeming friends who undermine your effort to be a writer. Stay close to those who encourage you. Most important of all, trust your own instincts about the people in your life. It is most likely that you are right about them.

# 34. TA CHUANG

*The Power of Great Style*

*Style is in no way a decoration as some people believe;
it is not even a matter of technique; it is — as color
is with painters — a quality of vision, the revelation
of the particular universe which each of us sees,
and which others do not see.*

— MARCEL PROUST

*It is the density of style which counts.
Through Hemingway's style you feel matter, iron, wood.*

— BORIS PASTERNAK

## COMMENTARY

Thunder coming out of heaven means that you may proceed too quickly when you add the stylistic flourishes your work requires. You let your powerful voice overshadow the simple, quiet stylistic revisions you should be implementing. This hexagram signifies the importance of keeping your own abilities in perspective; do not ever step away from what is just or right.

## PREDICTION

With sufficient self-knowledge, you will slow down and do a great job of revising your work for stylistic concerns.

## ADVISORY

You are in a rush to perfect your work and revise your style. There is danger that you will not wait for the right time to put the final touches on your work-in-progress. Slow down and do not let your power as a writer over-shadow your knowledge of what is right to do. Do justice to your manuscript by proceeding with patience and insight.

## FOR THE WRITER

Write in a totally new style. Write a poem in which you mix common clichés with more insightful writings. Play with enjambment (see Glossary, p. 277) to make readers look at these clichés in a new way.

## MOVING LINES

Nine at the beginning means that you are likely to proceed by forcing your work into a new style. Using force in this way is certain to lead to disaster. Take a page you have already written and revise it stylistically into a poem that sounds very different from how you usually sound. Then put it back into words you would ordinarily use. Which is better?

Nine in the second place means that you will find

good fortune if you persevere in your usual way of polishing your writing. Beware of too much self-confidence, however. Take a page you have already written and turn it into a poem written in a new voice but with familiar vocabulary.

Nine in the third place means that you must not boast about your writing prowess, or misfortune will follow. Instead, persevere silently in revising your writing for style; let others question you without showing irritation. Write a short poem in the voice of someone you really love.

Nine in the fourth place means you will no longer feel remorseful about something you have done. You will go on working quietly and with steady effort until you have achieved success. Write a poem in which you change all the verbs to more active ones.

Six in the fifth place means you should give up any obnoxious behavior that you cling to. Notice what is causing your misfortune, and you will ultimately achieve success. Write a poem in which you question authority.

Six at the top means you can go neither forward nor back in your writing. You must stay exactly where you are, improving the page you are working on and waiting for the best moment to continue beyond that page. Write a poem in which you explore what it means to be frozen and static.

### LAST WORD

Great style is learned, not assumed.

# 35. Chin

## *Progress*

*The opening scene dominated the book, set the tone,
and then, of course, as I worked on it I had to write the
book — that is, create scenes, encounters, and so on.*

— ELIZABETH HARDWICK

*The typewriter had a rhythm, made a music of its own
I don't mean the script I mean the typewriter.
In those complicated sentences I rarely left anything out.
And I got up a tremendous speed.*

— ALICE B. TOKLAS

## COMMENTARY

The sun rises over the earth and all is natural and fine.
You emerge from the dark and find the way that has
been in front of you all along. You are no longer clouded
by contact with people and other writers who slow your
progress.

## PREDICTION

You will shake off the past and find your way through
the present with real elegance and clarity.

### ADVISORY

Be on the lookout for a writer who is superior to you and who offers help. He or she will be of immense aid and should be properly welcomed into your life.

### FOR THE WRITER

Write a letter to yourself in which you emphasize the past, present, and future of your work-in-progress. Write about what you have already done, how you feel right now about what you have done, and what you might do with it in the future.

### MOVING LINES

Six at the beginning means you are progressing well but will suffer a minor setback. Stay the course. Write a letter to yourself (which you can read at a later time, as necessary) in which you offer yourself encouragement in difficult times.

Six in the second place means you will make good progress, but it will be a time of sorrow. Keep persevering through that sorrow and success will be yours. Write a short letter in which you console yourself in times of trouble.

Six in the third place means that all involved are in harmony. No regrets. Write a short letter to yourself in which you lay out your life's aims as a writer.

Nine in the fourth place means there is a risk of your acquiring too many books, pads, writing instruments — things that weigh you down when you should be studying your craft. Travel more lightly. Write a short letter to yourself in which you caution yourself against getting distracted by material consumption.

Six in the fifth place means that good fortune will come. You will find yourself as a writer and proceed with great luck. Write a short letter to yourself in which you talk about what dreams you have already achieved as a writer.

Nine at the top means you will have to take the offensive in doing your own work. You will have to assert your right to time, materials, and a place to do your work. Write a short letter to yourself outlining what you need in order to successfully do your work. Display the letter where you write.

## LAST WORD

Overall, this hexagram is propitious. You must continue your work because it will ultimately be successful. There may be some real obstacles ahead, but good fortune follows.

# 36. Ming I

*Overcome Writing Difficulties*

*I couldn't even read a newspaper article. . . . I'd start, then lay it aside, and after a while I realized I had been laying things aside for months. I think it's being shocked and losing the ability to concentrate. It was like losing a solace or a haven. After about six months, it started coming back, and I'm okay now.*

— MAXINE HONG KINGSTON

*It seems to me that in my youth there was work, an integral part of life which illuminated everything else in it. Now it is something I have to fight for.*

— BORIS PASTERNAK

## COMMENTARY

The name of this hexagram may be translated as "wounding of the bright." You are falling into difficulty and trouble as you keep trying to compose. You have two choices ahead: to receive help from friends or to do harm to an older man. Obviously, the former is preferable.

## PREDICTION

You are going to hit difficult times in your writing process. If you accept help from friends, then and only then will you make progress.

## ADVISORY

As you compose, be cautious. The most important task ahead is for you to keep lit your inner light. Darkness is going to fall around you, so you need that bright light that is yours alone, as well as the help of friends. Unexpected friends and old friends will probably appear to aid you with your writing. Persevere in the process and do not despair. All things are impermanent.

## FOR THE WRITER

Sit somewhere comfortable and close your eyes. Center yourself. After a few moments, when you have centered yourself, write down the recipe for a potion that will cure you of your depression. Use unconventional ingredients.

## MOVING LINES

Nine at the beginning means you will not find sustenance for your work for three days, three weeks, or three months. You must know that your enthusiasm and abilities will return. Write down a spell that you can say, and use it when you are frozen with inability to progress.

Six in the second place means that despite wounds

(especially a wound to the thigh), darkness, and unhap-piness, you will rise above the darkness. Good fortune. Write down the cure for lasting darkness.

Nine in the third place means that chance is at work. You must work against the darkness that sur-rounds you without expecting quick results. Write a spell for maintaining strength in lasting darkness.

Six in the fourth place means that you understand fully the forces arrayed against you. You leave before the storm fully breaks. Write down a ritual to be performed if darkness surrounds you.

Six in the fifth place means you will have to take extraordinary measures to overcome the darkness. In ancient times, this meant feigning insanity. You must persevere, whatever your strategy. Write a spell in which you overcome the darkness.

Six at the top means that darkness rises and then falls away. Darkness eventually consumes itself and light returns. Good fortune. Write a ritual in which light is invited to return.

## LAST WORD

You inhabit a dangerous place. Proceed very cautiously, if at all. Know that the darkness is temporary, that all things pass on. Light shall return to you, and your writ-ing will prosper.

# 37. Chia Jên

*Write What You Know*

*The business of the poet is not to find new emotions,*
*but to use the ordinary ones.*

— T. S. ELIOT

*The style of a poet is nothing more than the personality*
*expressed in his bodily gestures; since poems themselves are*
*bodily gestures, they will naturally express this personality*
*as well as the way the poet dresses or lights his cigarette.*
*But since poems are bodies themselves, they will also express*
*their own unique personalities, related to but distinct from*
*the poet's. It is true that the poet speaks the poem, but the*
*poem also speaks itself, and this is because it is a body.*

— JOHN VERNON

## COMMENTARY

This hexagram recommends an orderly arrangement
of person, family, home, community, and state as a
whole. To maintain order, self-knowledge is required
and the right role expected. For the writer, this hexagram indicates that words will have meaning only when
they spring from the familiar, the ordinary — when they

arise from your own person. In the terms of the I Ching, that is when all is in order and flame rises from its fuel naturally.

## PREDICTION

You will learn to write what you know, and that writing will be successful.

## ADVISORY

You should write about what is familiar. If you do this, you, your writing, and your immediate community will be nurtured.

## FOR THE WRITER

Think back to the first community to which you belonged (city, town, suburb, country; school, place of worship; sport, club, special interest group). What brought that community together? What were its shared values, subjects of gossip, points of contention? How did it feel to be part of it? Write either a short poem or a work of prose in which you answer some of these questions.

## MOVING LINES

Nine at the beginning means that you must know yourself and write about what you find there. Write a short work in which you analyze yourself as though you were a community of mind, body, and soul.

Six in the second place means that you should stick to the familiar in all that you write. Your place is to write only what you know. Write a short work in which you analyze the community operating within the house, apartment building, family, or group of friends within which you live.

Nine in the third place means that if you are too severe in following what you know, success will follow nevertheless. But if you dally and are happy as you seek the topic with which you are most familiar, distress follows. Write a short work in which you explore the subjects that you know the most about. What are you an expert in?

Six in the fourth place means that your well-being is assured when you order your writing around what you know best. Order your writing space, schedule, and instruments in the way that assures your best work. Write a short work in which you explore what it means to feel well-being. What contributes to that feeling?

Nine in the fifth place means that you needn't fear that writing only about what you know will lead to a boring or unsuccessful outcome. Each person's intimate knowledge is another person's surprising discovery. Much is to be taught, and much learned. Write a short work in which you describe a household ritual that you observe nearly every day, sometimes more than once a day.

Nine at the top means that if you write about what you know, good fortune will follow. Your work will command respect. Write a short work in which you explain everything you know about clouds or stars.

## LAST WORD

To write what you know is to know yourself. And to know yourself is to place an implicit demand on you to order yourself — your thoughts, your dreams, your desires. To have an orderly mind does not mean to have an uncreative mind. To write about what is familiar, to develop an orderly mind, is to routinely see the extraordinary in the ordinary.

# 38. K'UEI

*Revision*

*[R]evision was always done manually. I preferred
yellow paper because it's not so responsible looking,
and I would just let fly and then put the thing away
after it was written and not look at it until the next day.
Then go to work on it with a pencil — chop and change
and then copy that off again on the yellow paper — and
this would go on for days sometimes. There are some
instances, especially in later work, when there have
been something like twenty versions of a poem.*

— CONRAD AIKEN

*When revising, I'm capable of replacing entire pages
with an asterisk and moving emphatically through time.
It comes with the territory — dispensing with what's
unnecessary, however much you like it.*

— ANN BEATTIE

## COMMENTARY

There are some juxtapositions in your writing that are
not quite right. This hexagram signals opposition. In
revising small parts of your work, you will enjoy success.
But in revising whole sections of your work, it is best to

pay attention. Figure out where the different parts properly belong. Resolve oppositions within your work by placing like with like. Metaphorically speaking, fire and water must be kept separate. Pour water into water, light fire with fire. In your scenes and stanzas, make voices consistent; put whole character descriptions together in one place; don't break apart your descriptions of setting into two or three parts; don't use three or four metaphors to describe the same thing.

## PREDICTION

You will revise your work and it will grow better, especially when you pay close attention to individual moments in your manuscript. You will learn how to write with care for all your characters and voices — and for yourself.

## ADVISORY

Be careful when you revise your work under the influence of this hexagram. It signifies difficulty with opposites. In regard to your writing, it might mean that you must smooth out the rough cuts in your work. Perhaps there is a sharp difference of opinion in your household about when or where you should write. Or perhaps there is a conflict in your revision technique. Preserve the individuality of your writing while reconciling the opposite impulses of your work.

## FOR THE WRITER

Read your work aloud with a pencil in your hand. Put a checkmark in the margin of any line in which you stop or stumble in your reading. Go back and revise those places. If you don't stumble anywhere in reading aloud, add three sentences.

## MOVING LINES

Nine at the beginning means you will avoid mistakes as you try to reconcile opposites. Proceed cautiously, and in the face of evil influences simply step aside; they will withdraw of their own accord. Take out a page of your writing and add three lines that help set the atmosphere. Keep adding three lines until you are through.

Nine in the second place means that there will be misunderstandings as you attempt to reconcile opposites. Revise a couple of pages you have already written by circling entire sentences (or lines) that you wish to revise. Copy them out on a separate piece of paper and start fresh with each one. Revise according to sound and imagery, maintaining consistency in both.

Six in the third place means that the attempt to reconcile opposites is a disaster at the beginning but comes, eventually, to a good end. You will not know how to proceed at first, but if you are true to yourself and your immediate company, the affair will resolve itself well. Revise a couple of pages by first reenvisioning their subject. Is there some other angle that might be better? When you are ready, attempt to rewrite this section from this new angle.

Nine in the fourth place means that you will feel isolated, even among friends. There is some danger here, probably because of your isolation, that is only averted by a close connection with a true friend. Revise two or three pages by inserting the voice of someone unexpected into the scene or poem.

Six in the fifth place means you will meet a stranger who will turn out to be a good friend. Such a friend helps you cope with isolation, estrangement, psychic wounds. Revise part of your work by circling those bits that are most problematic to you. Try writing next to each one what your aim is in including it. Why are these words there at all? Explain it to yourself. Then attempt to revise those parts.

Nine at the top means that you will not recognize your own best friend — at least not at first. You will fail to reconcile opposites because you are not seeing either one clearly. To be successful, you must wipe your lenses clean and see afresh and true. Revise two or three pages of your work by adding an image that stands in for the emotional tension of the scene. Add an ordinary object whose characteristics reveal something about the larger story or lyric.

## LAST WORD

Where do opposites occur in your writing life? Identify those places, then look clearly at where the opposition arises. What is the crux, the stasis, the moment of tension? Once the two horns of the dilemma have been described, it is easier to plan a strategy for their reconciliation. Choose your strategy wisely. Then rearrange your writing life as you can to make it more productive and satisfying.

# 39. CHIEN

*Move Ahead Despite Obstructions*

*Sometimes I believe these books are already written
and my job is simply to allow them to come through me.
My job is to get out of my own way so that I can let the
process take care of me. But that's scary stuff.*

— SUE GRAFTON

*The central message in all mythology, in all portions
of history, in all the world, is that there are ways,
such as dreaming, to tap into the wild side of us,
which is where all the richness and all the healing
and all the creativity comes from. We've managed
to shut it off completely, most of us, in this modern day,
and it can cripple us badly. Very, very badly.*

— ANNE RIVERS SIDDONS

## COMMENTARY

The image of this hexagram is of a wide abyss before you
and a steep mountain just behind you. There is no easy
egress. Nevertheless, the fact that the mountain is still
gives a hint of how you might escape such a seemingly

intransigent situation. The inferior person attributes all difficulties to the influence of other people. The superior person, when faced with difficulties, seeks the error in himself. Find people of like mind and search for a leader who will lead all of you back across the mountain. By holding tight to your sense of inner purpose, you will overcome all obstacles.

## PREDICTION

Your writing will thrive despite the obstacle right in front of you today. Work hard on modifying your own character and outlook, and your writing will steadily improve.

## ADVISORY

Surround yourself with other artists and writers who are trying to develop their work — and their character. Recognize the links between yourself as a writer and the writing you do. Keeping your mind clear will keep your writing clear. Seek the obstacle inside yourself to overcome before you worry about overcoming the obstacle outside.

## FOR THE WRITER

Write a one-page monologue in the voice of a part of your body that hurts right now, that has been injured in the past, or that is just plain uncomfortable in its life. Write three lines in response from another part of your body.

## MOVING LINES

Six at the beginning means that you must consider the best time to face the obstacle that lies before you. Retreat until you are clear in strategy and intention. Write a one-page monologue in the voice of the obstacle that faces you. Know thine enemy.

Six in the second place means that you must identify the obstacle and walk out to meet it head-on. You are bound by your attachment to writing to seek the dangers that might lie ahead. Write a one-page monologue in which you explain your dedication to writing no matter how much it hurts sometimes.

Nine in the third place means that going ahead will result in disaster. The correct response is to wait until the right moment to strike. Write a one-page monologue in which you speculate on what is hardest about being a writer.

Six in the fourth place means that you cannot handle the situation alone. You must seek allies and defeat the obstacle together. Write a one-page monologue that is a call to arms. Call all your friends to help you overcome an obstacle.

Nine in the fifth place means that friends arrive to help you overcome the obstacle. By coordinating your efforts, you and your friends successfully overcome the obstacle. Write a one-page monologue in which you talk about your friends' great abilities at times like this.

Six at the top means you should not give up on this world and take refuge in a spiritual retreat or in the worlds beyond this one. You can rescue yourself from adversity by returning to the tumult of daily life and seeking the help of an important friend. Write a one-page monologue in which you plead with someone close to you to help you overcome an obstacle.

## LAST WORD

There are obstructions before and in front of you. They must be taken with great seriousness. However, it is clear that with the help of friends you may renew your dedication to your craft and overcome these great obstacles. Stay calm, plan your strategy, gauge your timing, then seek to join friends in overcoming any obstacle, however great.

# 40. Hsieh

*Work on the Ending*

*Reading is a pleasure, but to finish reading, to come
to the blank space at the end, is also a pleasure.*

— JOHN ASHBERY

*As I'm getting towards the end of a story, the ending that,
during my waking hours, I think will happen is
sometimes subverted or obliterated by [a] dream.
It happens just as I'm getting ready to write that scene.*

— BHARATI MUKHERJEE

## COMMENTARY

Haste brings good fortune as one approaches the ending. In other words, it is important to draft the ending and return to the rest of the manuscript as quickly as possible. While haste toward the end promises to bring good results, it is also important to return to the daily work of revising, rewriting, and reenvisioning the manuscript as a whole. Return to the ordinary tasks of writing as quickly as possible.

## PREDICTION

If you choose to work on the ending of your piece now, you will find success waiting there.

## ADVISORY

Draft the ending of your work rather quickly. Generate the shape and ideas of your ending without thinking too much about it. Then do not dwell on the mistakes that are there, but pass over them. Let your pen work like fresh water, washing away some of the mistakes or missteps that are part of that draft. Don't hesitate to ask for help from a friend after you have the first draft done.

## FOR THE WRITER

Find a photograph of a person or people. Write two pages in which you describe what that person did immediately following the taking of that picture. Then write three different sentences, each of which could function as an end to the description. Choose the best ending, revise it, and add it to your two pages.

## MOVING LINES

Six at the beginning means that few words are needed. All is at rest, peaceful, and still — and you are ready to write. Write two pages in which you describe a photograph of someone recuperating in a hospital bed.

Nine in the second place means that there will be distractions in the process of writing an ending. Keep focused, attack the task wholeheartedly, and the ending will be fine. Write two pages in which you describe a photograph of a silver fox running.

Six in the third place means that your ending should be clear and strong. You should not be like the man who carried a pack on his back for the whole time he sat in a carriage. Do not be careless. Write two pages in which you describe a photograph of a man being robbed.

Nine in the fourth place means you must find true friends to help you write your ending. You will be surrounded by flatterers and sycophants, all of whom you must shake off. When you compose your ending, be sure the people around you are hardy and true. Write two pages in which you describe a photograph of a man's clear eyes as he sets off on an important journey.

Six in the fifth place means that you must set yourself apart from people who would weaken you as you write the ending to your manuscript. You may have to end some relationships as well as ending your text. Write two pages in which you describe a dusty road with one traveler on it.

Six at the top means that the ending you write will be very good. Not only will it pull together the whole work, but it will suggest ways to further the entire project beautifully. Write two pages in which you describe a hawk circling over his prey.

## LAST WORD

It is hard for writers (and most artists) to end the relationship with a work-in-progress. Writers who have trouble ending relationships in general will have an even more painful time with ending a manuscript. This hexagram acknowledges the difficulties of separating from a long work, and also suggests that work on the ending will be favorable.

# 41. Sun

*Shorten Your Writing*

*I love form. It makes you cut down.*

— MAY SARTON

*Writing is a kind of free fall that you then go back and edit and shape.*

— ALLAN GURGANUS

## COMMENTARY

Decrease — revise your work by shortening it. Decrease the number of words, the momentum of the piece, the number of scenes or lines. Although you decrease with seriousness, the net effect will be for your work to lose nothing of substance. The quality of your writing will increase because you shorten and sharpen it. Your community of readers will appreciate your tightening the text.

## PREDICTION

By shortening the text, your work will grow substantially better.

## ADVISORY

Look closely at your work-in-progress. If you are writing prose, revise parts that have long descriptions of settings and characters, that build extended lyrical interludes, or that forecast the narrative instead of retaining a little suspense. If you are writing poetry, revise parts that repeat images, metaphors, or lyrics (except when the returning chorus is there by design). In both cases, reading your own work aloud — or, even better, having a friend read it aloud to you — will help you identify those places that are wordy. Read the original and the revision aloud to make sure your efforts are well executed.

## FOR THE WRITER

Write a short monologue from the point of view of a crow. Then draw a line in the margin next to every word, phrase, sentence, or paragraph that you think is essential to the work. Discard everything else and read aloud what you have left. Is it enough? Restore just as much of the original text as you need to make the draft coherent.

## MOVING LINES

Nine at the beginning means to go quickly as you shorten your text. Don't second-guess yourself; progress without hesitation. Write a short monologue from the point of view of a rabbi, then perform the same exercise described in "For the Writer."

Nine in the second place means that as you shorten your text you will expand someone else's sense of self. Proceed cautiously as you revise your text; the possibility of misfortune is there. Write a short monologue from the point of view of a minister, then perform the exercise described in "For the Writer."

Six in the third place means that three people will be involved in shortening your text, if you decide to seek outside help. If you decide to do all the revising by yourself, you will find yourself with an unexpected companion before you are through. Write a short monologue from the point of view of a hermit, then proceed as described in "For the Writer."

Six in the fourth place means that you must develop more humility as you work on your text. If you practice genuine humility, you will share joy with others near to you. Write a short monologue from the point of view of a child around eleven, and then proceed as described in "For the Writer."

Six in the fifth place means that good fortune will arrive no matter what. You need fear nothing as you revise and shorten your text. Write a short monologue from the point of view of a wizard, then proceed as described in "For the Writer."

Nine at the top means that your work will benefit others a great deal. As you shorten your work, pay attention to who will be affected by your words. Write a short monologue from the point of view of a priest, then proceed as described in "For the Writer."

## LAST WORD

If you shorten your text with care and commitment, readers will benefit. It is recommended that you seek the help of others as you revise. Whatever your method, tighten your work and it will improve.

# 42. I

## *Expand Your Text*

*I think what happens, really, is that when you're writing,*
*part of the process is mysterious. You can plot out things*
*and it's all conscious, you can do that and make*
*decisions about what characters you want to have.*
*And then you stop and you just trust instinct and you*
*don't know where a certain thing will come from.*

— CHARLES JOHNSON

*It's all done with words, words, words.*

— WILLIAM EVERSON

## COMMENTARY

Wind above and thunder below; the two elements reinforcing, strengthening, and increasing each other. They indicate the need to expand one's work, to increase the number of words and pages, to pay more attention in the current manuscript. This time will not last forever, so it is important to begin expanding your work quickly — without sacrificing quality.

## PREDICTION

You will increase the degree of detail, the number of words or pages, the amount of attention paid, or the level of development in your work to good result.

## ADVISORY

Proceed with some degree of speed, because this hexagram indicates that the time in which to expand your text is fleeting. As you expand your work, it is necessary to expand yourself as well. You must look inside yourself and be as generous as you know how — to yourself and to others. Imitate men and women who are good; find parts of yourself that are small or stingy, and pull them out by the root.

## FOR THE WRITER

Write a character sketch (see Glossary, p. 277) of a living relative you feel close to. Draw this person's picture at the top of the page if it will help you remember his or her characteristics. When you are finished writing, go back through the draft and add at least one detail related to each of the five senses; tell us one additional thing about how he or she smells, tastes, feels, sounds, or looks.

If you prefer to work on your current writing project, add the same kind of details to each page.

## MOVING LINES

Nine at the beginning means you will achieve the very highest good fortune. Great help will come from an important person, and you will discover new meanings to the instruction "expand your writing." Write a character sketch (see Glossary, p. 277) of the most important person you know. When you are done, revise the work by adding five-sense imagery (see Glossary, p. 278).

Six in the second place means that if you persevere in developing your text, you will have good fortune. Further, you will do something for the good of the world. Write a character sketch (see Glossary, p. 277) of the most noble person you know. When you are done, revise the work by adding five-sense imagery (see Glossary, p. 278).

Six in the third place means that your good intentions may end in misfortune. Try to expand your text, and if you act in harmony with the shape and feeling of the existing text, good fortune will ensue. Write a character sketch (see Glossary, p. 277) of someone who has survived unfortunate events. When you are done, revise the work by adding five-sense imagery (see Glossary, p. 278).

Six in the fourth place means that you will need someone's help to mediate between you and your work. Your work will wish not to be changed, while you know it must be altered and expanded to bring it to its best aspect. Balance these opposing views. Write a character sketch (see Glossary, p. 277) of a professional person (e.g., lawyer, professor, teacher, businessperson), then expand the sketch by adding five-sense imagery (see Glossary, p. 278).

Nine in the fifth place means you will find supreme good fortune. Don't look for reasons to expand your work, but simply do it — from the depths of your kind heart. Write a character sketch (see Glossary, p. 277) of a person who has the warmest heart you know. Then, add five-sense imagery (see Glossary, p. 278).

Nine at the top means that you are not able to expand your work, hard though you may try. You must develop an attitude in harmony with your work's needs, or you will suffer misfortune. Write a character sketch (see Glossary, p. 277) of someone you know who is dishonest. When you are finished, add five-sense imagery (see Glossary, p. 278).

## LAST WORD

It is extremely important that you examine your work closely and find the places where it needs to be expanded. At the same time, you must examine yourself closely, looking at those places where you could be kinder or more compassionate. Working with writing is the same as working with yourself; know the shape of both.

# 43. KUAI

## *Writer's Block Overcome*

*At that period I thought I'd dried up completely. I hadn't written anything for some time and was rather desperate.*

— T. S. ELIOT

*I don't think you can write a poem for more than two hours. After that you're going round in circles, and it's much better to leave it for twenty-four hours, by which time your subconscious or whatever has solved the block and you're ready to go on.*

— PHILIP LARKIN

## COMMENTARY

This hexagram signifies breaking through some sort of trouble or difficulty, like a river breaking through a dam. Writer's block is overcome by perseverance in the face of danger. You do not carry on the struggle by force or by an instrument of battle. Instead, you bring resoluteness to the struggle. Through perseverance and the goodness of your character, you will break through writer's block.

## PREDICTION

You will break through writer's block.

## ADVISORY

Difficulties like writer's block are a matter of forgetting one's talents. What do you gain by having writer's block? How does it benefit you or your writing? The best way to overcome your writer's block is to emphasize all the ways in which you are already a fluent writer. Remember your talents as a writer. Remember your own good character. And recall that if you put pen to paper and write, you are a writer.

## FOR THE WRITER

Get up and walk around. Fix yourself a beverage — tea, water, a soft drink, something caffeinated, something not, whatever you like. Find something to write with. Then settle somewhere comfortable. Write a sentence about your surroundings. Then describe at least one object in great detail. Move on to your clothing. What are you wearing? Write it down. Is anything uncomfortable, particularly colorful or dark, too big or too small? Write it down. Continue writing about everything you see, smell, taste, or hear until you have written two pages. Cross out and erase nothing. Turn the page when you are done and turn to your own writing project.

## MOVING LINES

Nine at the beginning means that you should not force yourself to get over writer's block too quickly. That would be a mistake. Instead, take your time, take small step after small step, and you will not make mistakes. Write a short essay about the first time you began some activity.

Nine in the second place means you should fear absolutely nothing. Readiness is everything. Write a short essay in which you discuss the ways in which you are rational or reasonable.

Nine in the third place means you should make friends with your writer's block. If the writer's block were a person, what would he or she be like? Write a short essay in which you describe your writer's block as a person speaking to you.

Nine in the fourth place means you will be obstinate in trying one single way to overcome writer's block. Instead, you should be relaxed and supple, trying several ways to overcome writer's block. This advice, however, is almost sure to be ignored. Write a short essay in which you describe writer's block as one team in a tug-of-war. You are the sole member of the opposing team. What is it like to tug the rope against writer's block?

Nine in the fifth place means that writer's block will be easily removed, but will return frequently. Do not be deflected from the course. Write a short essay in which you describe a contemporary Hydra — a creature who grows two new heads for every one that you chop off.

Six at the top means that, despite your best efforts, misfortune arrives. But that's okay. Just keep working steadily to come to terms with your writer's block, understanding what you gain from it as much as what you lose by it. Write a short essay in which you describe someone who entered a contest and came very close to having the winning entry.

## LAST WORD

Writer's block is an affliction that can be slight or deadly, short-term or long-term, real or assumed. If you have writer's block, it means that you are being slow to put words on paper. You need to understand yourself thoroughly, to look inside your own character and seek to know what you gain by acting this way. Writer's block ultimately is a block in yourself, some sort of hesitation or halt in the way your life is progressing. To overcome writer's block is to overcome the habits of self. Good luck.

# 44. Kou

*Beware of Misfortune*

*There is no innocent literature.*

— JEAN-PAUL SARTRE

*I walked into the house, sat down at the typewriter with my hat still on my head, and wrote a page, a sort of rough statement of the book I meant to write, which I then thumb-tacked to a shelf and didn't look at again until it was finished. To my surprise, everything I had managed to do in the novel was on that page. But in general the thing creeps along slowly, like a mole in the dark.*

— WILLIAM MAXWELL

## COMMENTARY

This hexagram signifies difficult times, immediate misfortune, or misguided aims. It is a situation that must be immediately met with countermeasures. You are at risk from someone or something dishonest in your life. The situation is dangerous.

## PREDICTION

Take immediate action to remove yourself from comrades who are dishonest, angry, or unreasonable, or you will be in grave danger.

## ADVISORY

Look over what you have already written. Are there parts of it that are unscrupulous or dishonest? Erase those parts and write again with greater honesty. Then look over the people in your life; are there some who are unkind, disgraceful, or dishonest? Root out the bad in both writing and social life, and you will have some small hope of escaping the darkness and evil that threaten.

## FOR THE WRITER

Charles Dickens is said to have had a ritual of touching certain objects on his desk three times before he began to write each day. What are your rituals, talismans, good luck symbols, things you say or do or touch to keep the writing gods happy? Write down at least three talismans, sayings, or objects that keep your writing flowing. Below each description, explain what powers or intentions each good luck symbol represents. Then be sure to undertake the rituals they suggest.

## MOVING LINES

Six at the beginning means that some danger will creep into your life, which you will underestimate because it

seems so small and weak at first. Vigorously oppose any
danger that enters your life, no matter how small. Write
a description of rituals you could undertake to rid your
writing space of bad energy or unpleasant associations.
Make part of the ritual a rhyming chant.

Nine in the second place means that, while there is
no one to blame, you must be very careful not to
encounter the evil that is already present. If you touch
the evil element, its aspects will spring forth in all their
color and liveliness. Write a description of a ritual you
could chant around a fire to get rid of a demon.

Nine in the third place means that the evil element
in your life will suddenly seem very tempting. Do not
join the evil, but resist it and continue to develop your
own good character. Write a description of someone or
something that is not good for you, but that is extremely
appealing nevertheless.

Nine in the fourth place means that misfortune is
near. It is important to maintain all genuine friendships,
even the ones that are more casual than substantive. You
will soon need all the friends you have. Write a description of the ideal friend.

Nine in the fifth place means that you must be
strong and forthright in your protection of your own
work — and the work of others. All writing is tremendously hard, and it is important that you recognize its
difficulty and teach others to respect that difficulty, too.
Write a description of a strong man who protects someone or something less strong — a cat, a friend, or a
child, for example.

Nine at the top means you will be tempted to

withdraw from the world. The daily world with its quo-
tidian concerns and meaningless rules and rituals may
suddenly seem too ridiculous to care about. Write a
description of a man or woman who cannot shake the
feeling that there is something wrong with the world.

## LAST WORD

It is difficult to warn against nearby danger when, in
fact, there is no immediate evidence of how dangerous
the world is to you. Again, jettison those so-called
friends who are behaving in an untoward manner, and
strike out on your own if necessary.

# 45. Ts'ui

*Form a Writing Group*

*I need to do things outside of my writing*
*— to bring people together not just in my imagination*
*but in real life in one room.*

— MAXINE HONG KINGSTON

*... that [writing] group was my education.*
*I knew individual writers, poems, and books through*
*them. I was exposed to the liveliness and range of the talk*
*and the wrangle of the argument... But most of all I got*
*the feeling that poetry was a vital activity...*

— ROBERT PENN WARREN

## COMMENTARY

When you form a writing group, success will come. Bringing food and drink to the writing group will improve the chances of success. Listen well to each other, and pay attention less to the words of famous writers and more to each other. The group will integrate well. Finally, be prepared for the unexpected.

## PREDICTION

If you form a writing group and are careful to pick reliable, responsible, enjoyable people, success is yours.

## ADVISORY

Write a list of the characteristics that your ideal writing group would have. What would the group be called? What would be its primary tasks? How many people would be in your ideal group? Who do you know who might fit this constellation of people and skills? When you form your writing group, you must gather people who are sympathetic in temperament and capable in their work. Agree on the rules of the group together: when people will exchange work, how copies will be made, the kinds of feedback being asked for. Initially the group will need a leader, who will have to be you.

## FOR THE WRITER

Imagine a combination of four or more famous writers sitting in a circle and discussing a manuscript written by one of them. Write out their conversation in the form of a play. What are the characteristics that you like about the conversation?

## MOVING LINES

Six at the beginning means that, if you are sincere in your plans and efforts, your group will coalesce and will probably be successful. No blame if the group fails, but members are likely to ask for help before that happens. Be prepared to respond. Write down a conversation (in the form of a play) among four writers, one of whom is you.

Six in the second place means that you should bring even just a small thing to the first meeting of your group. You might offer food or drink, a small gift, or an introduction of each member, emphasizing each person's skills as a writer. Write down a conversation in the form of a play, in which you give a gift to the other three writers in your group and you all talk about it.

Six in the third place means there will be some initial reluctance among writers in the group to talking sincerely about writing. This is a mistake, and may be linked to the fact that you are not yet a community. Write down a conversation in the form of a play in which you and three other writers discuss the rules of the writing group.

Nine in the fourth place means that there will be great success in your writing group. This success will come because you, as leader, will work tirelessly to make sure that community forms and that the comments among group members are sincere. Write down a conversation between two writers in the form of a play, in which the group leader is one of the characters and talks about his or her efforts to shape the group.

Nine in the fifth place means that not all members of the group are yet sincere about the work. Perseverance among all members is required, so that over time community builds and the work is shared appropriately. Write down a conversation between two writers in which one writer is hesitant to give honest responses and the other writer is helping him or her be more sincere.

Six at the top means that there will be grief in the group. There will be some tears, but do not ally yourself with the grieving person alone. Write down a conversation among the four members of the group, in which one member grows very upset and you have to figure out together how to handle the problem.

### LAST WORD

All groups are difficult to manage, and each member typically takes on her own role or persona, over time. Your job as founder of the group is simply to introduce the members and coordinate a discussion of how to proceed. Do not ally yourself with any one member of the group, but do your best to be evenhanded. Proceed patiently and slowly, giving time for the community to coalesce, and your group will probably become a successful place to discuss writing-in-progress.

# 46. Shêng

*Achievement Is Near*

*You write a book and it's like putting a message in a bottle
and throwing it in the ocean. You don't know
if it will ever reach any shore. And there, you see,
sometimes it falls in the hands of the right person.*

— ISABEL ALLENDE

*My advice to beginning writers is that a large part of
writing is simply to stay with a project. Every story, every
novel has to be completed before I move on to the next one.
I'm very single-minded, very obsessive.*

— T. CORAGHESSAN BOYLE

## COMMENTARY

You will progress from obscurity to influence, from solitude to having your work read by a group (of what size is not clear). Your work will grow in prominence and power. Take care to develop the final drafts of your work without hurry and with confidence. They will reward your care.

## PREDICTION

Your work will be successful.

## ADVISORY

Do not hurry as you put the finishing touches on your manuscript. Take it slow and easy, because that way will lead to near-certain success. Do not pause in your efforts, but also do not be sloppy or quick. Enjoy the process. Then your audience is sure to enjoy it, too.

## FOR THE WRITER

Write a short sketch about an equestrian statue that comes to life, runs in the Kentucky Derby, and wins.

## MOVING LINES

Six at the beginning means that great success follows slow effort. Be sure to proceed steadily and with confidence, and polish your work with care. Write a short sketch about a horse who grows from a pony into a great racehorse.

Nine in the second place means that you should be sincere and bring a small gift to anyone who is helping you with your writing. Your solid character helps you polish your work with sincerity. Write a short sketch about a horse who has a special gift.

Nine in the third place means that you revise and polish your work, only to find that there is no audience for the finished piece. It is beautifully written, clear, and sincere, but no one is in the immediate vicinity to listen. Write a short skit about a horse who is one of the fastest horses in the country, but is unknown to the racing world.

Six in the fourth place means a powerful person will offer compliments about your accomplishments in writing. Polish your work with deep concentration, and your final work will be admired by someone famous or rich. Write a dramatic monologue (see Glossary, p. 277) from the point of view of a horse musing about his rich owner.

Six in the fifth place means that it is extremely important to be careful; persevere through the final revisions and polishing. Do not be distracted from the main work at hand by early success. Write a flash fiction (see Glossary, p. 278) about a Russian racehorse who grows overconfident before running in an important race.

Six at the top means that it will sometimes be dark and unclear as you put in your final revisions. Persevere anyway, and success will be yours. Write a short sketch about a horse who has to practice daily for two years before he is fit to run in any important races.

## LAST WORD

To polish one's work is hard. To let go of one's work, to call it finished, is even harder. When you do so, according to this hexagram you will achieve some recognition and success. Perseverance and steadiness are rewarded as you work to revise your work one last time.

# 47. K'UN

*Take a Short Rest*

*I should leave poems to lie, to be rescrawled,*
*and not be so eager to stick them in my book.*

— SYLVIA PLATH

*As a rule, with me an unfinished thing is a thing that*
*might as well be rubbed out. It's better, if there's something*
*good in it that I might make use of it elsewhere, to leave it*
*at the back of my mind than on paper in a drawer. If I*
*leave it in the drawer it remains the same thing, but if it's*
*in the memory it becomes transformed into something else.*

— T. S. ELIOT

## COMMENTARY

There is every sign that you are exhausted. Your creative
process is dried up, and you and your work are in a time
of adversity. It is very important that you take a short
rest to recharge yourself. Building your inner strength
and being of few words right now is the best way to proceed. Take care.

## PREDICTION

If you do not rest, you will fall into using empty words. If you do take a short rest, success awaits.

## ADVISORY

It is absolutely necessary that you slow down. Your creative abilities are gravely depleted right now. In the face of danger and nervous exhaustion, it is necessary to be relaxed, cheerful, and self-aware. Be kind to yourself and rest as necessary. Show others your mettle.

## FOR THE WRITER

Imagine where you would like to be on vacation right now. Write a two-page description of the place (and the people, if there are any) in minute detail. Put in one object or detail that is completely unexpected.

## MOVING LINES

Six at the beginning means that you are stuck in an oppressive mental state, which makes it difficult to write. It is most important that you develop inner strength in dealing with this oppression. Write a two-page description of a pleasant body of water you know; put yourself in that body of water and rejuvenate.

Nine in the second place means that you are experiencing depression and lack of focus in your writing. There are obstructions to your creative process that are not generated by external events. Write a two-page description of the place where you have been the happiest.

Six in the third place means that your bed is uncomfortable, your mind is restless, and your creative life feels unfulfilling. You are banging your head against a wall. Write a two-page description of an imaginary island where you would go to rejuvenate yourself.

Nine in the fourth place means that you have lost all speed and energy. You feel unnecessarily humiliated. Write a two-page description of a real sanctuary that would restore your heart and soul.

Nine in the fifth place means you are good-hearted even as you experience fatigue. You find little help or aid, but if you continue to develop strength of character and compassion, your ability to work will return to you. Write a two-page letter addressed to the sponsors of a contest. The letter should describe your dream vacation and explain why you are the best person to award a vacation to.

Six at the top means you are frozen in place, unable to write for fear of the consequences. You feel oppressed. Write a two-page analysis of why people get depressed and how vacations can help them feel better. Give yourself a vacation in your imagination. Write about that, too.

## LAST WORD

If you feel oppressed and gloomy, as this hexagram indicates, it is most important that you develop the strength of character to overcome such blues. Have inner strength of steel as you consider the situation. Be good to yourself as well as to others. Give yourself enough time to genuinely recharge and feel better.

# 48. Ching

*Face Your Writing Demons*

*I seemed to have lost my imagination.*
*Fiction takes compassion for other people, including*
*fictional characters, and I was wounded in such a way*
*that I didn't have energy to give to these imaginary people.*

— MAXINE HONG KINGSTON

*I may start a piece, find it obstructive, lack a way out,*
*and not complete the thing for a year, or years . . .*

— MARIANNE MOORE

## COMMENTARY

There are demons lurking beneath your writing process
— subtle creatures that speak out from the bottom of a
well. They can undermine your efforts or support your
desires to be authentic. These demons are unpredictable
and fickle, but not necessarily bad. Work with them as
much as you work against them, and you will benefit
from knowing them.

## PREDICTION

If you work hard to develop yourself inwardly, your demons will work for you and show you a necessary truth about yourself.

## ADVISORY

Working on one's writing demons means working on the self. As you develop ways to work with your own demons, take care to develop a concomitant compassion and generosity toward others. Working on the self always entails developing new attitudes and capacities for working with other people. As you face your demons, do not forget to face the truths of your existence, too.

## FOR THE WRITER

Write the first draft of a sestina (see Glossary, p. 281) in which each line refers to a demon, imaginary or real.

## MOVING LINES

Six at the beginning means you are mired in mud. Your creative work is feeling murky, and your sense of yourself is flawed and wandering. Write the first draft of a sestina about a person wandering through a swamp.

Nine in the second place means that you have good intentions but do not have the strength to see them through. Do not associate with people who are petty or dull. Write the first draft of a sestina about a person who falls into a friendship that is unworthy of him or her.

Nine in the third place means you have abilities and

capacities that no one knows about. The demons within are both positive and negative forces, but they do little harm nor good because they are unrecognized by you. Write the first draft of a sestina about a person of great ability who goes unrecognized in his daily life.

Six in the fourth place means that you must put yourself in order, making peace with your demons, before you turn any attention to others. Note where your strength lies and foster that strength. Write the first draft of a sestina about a person who puts all his effort into knowing himself.

Nine in the fifth place means that several different demons speak to you and work with you, and in many cases they are of great help. These demons are not evil or misplaced; they are simply spirits or winds that urge you in one direction or another. Write the first draft of a sestina in which you describe a superior person to whom you should be listening.

Six at the top means you will have great good fortune. The demons are neither forbidding nor lighthearted. They are evidence of an inner wealth, the value of which you are just beginning to comprehend. Write the first draft of a sestina about a rich woman who keeps growing richer.

## LAST WORD

As you develop your own character, your inner wealth grows and grows. The stronger you grow, the more deftness and sensitivity you will bring to working with your writing demons. Take care to develop the core of yourself so that you are well prepared to deal with your demons.

# 49. Ko

*Work on Transitions in Your Writing*

*. . . I found it hard to revise.*
*Cutting it down into small bits, I could work*
*on it much more carefully and make fast transitions.*

— ROBERT LOWELL

*In time, a writer, or any artist, stops making mistakes*
*on a crude, first level, and begins making mistakes*
*on the next, more elevated level. And then finally you*
*begin to make your mistakes on the highest level —*
*let's say the upper slopes of slippery Parnassus —*
*and it's at that point you need coaching.*

— JOHN BARTH

## COMMENTARY

One of the original translations of this hexagram refers to it as symbolizing "an animal's pelt," or any organic thing that metamorphoses over the course of a year. Different colors, different textures, different tendencies emerge and submerge over the course of several seasons. The spaces between colors or textures or tendencies are blurred, not separated or demarcated. This blurring is also known as a "transition," or a shift from color to color or texture to texture that is subtle and gradual rather than hard and abrupt.

## PREDICTION

As you progress through the seasons of your writing, you will find yourself moving back and forth between different aspects of your work with greater ease.

## ADVISORY

Note where you are paying too little attention to the larger arc of inner seasons within which we compose. Note, too, the relationship between inner transformation and outer transformation. Both the self and the world shift among capacities and character with growing subtlety and insight. In the case of your writing, pay close attention to where you change direction — as well as to the ways in which you gradually improve over time.

## FOR THE WRITER

In free verse (see Glossary, p. 278), write twenty or so lines about the first time you fell in love. Then go back over the free verse and draw a horizontal line between the lines wherever a break seems natural. Next, go back over the lines and cross out any words or phrases that feel unnecessary, cumbersome, repetitive. Finally, copy out the poem again, leaving a line of blank space between each informal "stanza" (the text between the horizontal lines you drew). If you wish, add some words to the first line of each stanza that serve as a transition or a signpost — that direct the reader to understand how the ideas, feelings, or images are connected.

## MOVING LINES

Nine at the beginning means that transitions should be made only when they are clearly needed. Do not rush into tinkering with the transitions between sections or paragraphs until it is absolutely necessary; let sleeping dogs lie. Write in free verse a short account of the first time you rode a bicycle. Start each stanza with a clear transition — a phrase or line that both looks back at what has been said and looks forward to what will be said.

Six in the second place means that transitions in your work are necessary. Add them if they are not already there. Write in free verse a short account of the first time you can remember doing something wrong. How did you know it was wrong? What did you do about it? Make sure to write transitions between all the stanzas in the poem.

Nine in the third place means that talk of making transitions (in individual lives as well as in a more general, global sense) will happen three times before you do anything. Ponder well what a transition means in your own life, then try to apply that new understanding of transitions to what you're doing now. Write in free verse a short account of the first time you drank alcohol, smoked a cigarette, or did something vaguely illicit.

Nine in the fourth place means that any feelings of regret you might have will soon disappear. Working on inner meaning and truth is still your most important task — still the only way in which genuine transitions will be crafted. Write in free verse a short account of the first time you realized that you wanted to be other than who people expected you to be. What skills did it take to be a nonconformist?

Nine in the fifth place means that you will be part of an evolving revolution, a substantial change in ways of thinking and doing that benefit all people. You will win the support of the people immediately around you. Write a short account in free verse of the first time you remember buying something by yourself.

Six at the top means that starting over brings misfortune. Developing a set of strategies and topics for future writing projects is key. Write a short account in free verse of the first school writing experience you can remember. Connect the experience to the present by writing about similarities between that first experience and a more recent one.

## LAST WORD

It is very important to remember that any shift in the external world is accompanied by a shift in the self or soul. Look deep within, and you will see the transitions not made, the projects not undertaken, the language of the self obscured and obscurant. When we speak of transitions, we are really talking about a kind of revolution, in which season yields to season and age yields to age. If you are going to be part of these cycles, it is important to know these changes as inevitable in the world, yourself, and your work. Use this knowledge wisely.

# 50. Ting

*Auspicious Refinement*

*[B]e aware of what the reader is feeling at any moment.
Maybe this is a no-brainer, but you need to ask yourself
what the reader knows — and what do they need to know.
It's essential to make a work of literature work.*

— KEITH KACHTICK

*Instead of simply pondering on a question, I will invent a
story that encompasses the question and try to see how it is
answered by people's reactions and their emotions.*

— NADINE GORDIMER

## COMMENTARY

Known as "the cauldron" in traditional translations of
the I Ching, Ting refers to a gentle kindling of flame
above (the upper trigram) from wind and wood below
(the lower trigram). There is an aspect of cooking or
making food in this hexagram, as well; Ting stands for
the nourishment that one human can offer to another.
Ting is also the reminder that visible and invisible are
inextricably linked; change in one leads to change in the

other. Finally, this hexagram is a message to writers, saying that the changes you make in your work are really changes in yourself.

### PREDICTION

There is power in your work, which is growing greater.

### ADVISORY

Go gently into the work you are currently doing. Let the wind increase and the fire steadily build, all on their own. Your work is steady and good; now you just need to let it build naturally.

### FOR THE WRITER

Write down a question that genuinely intrigues you — about life, a lover, meaning, logistics, places, imagination, creativity, or death. Then write the first page of a story that embodies that question.

### MOVING LINES

Six at the beginning means there will be a cleansing away of stagnant thoughts, deeds, work. You will continue to refine your writing so that it maintains liveliness and gains real authority. You will be recognized for the work you do. Write a page that embodies the question *Where is my mind located?*

Nine in the second place means that you will have good fortune. Some of your companions will envy your success, but you will know how to deal with them gently. You must concentrate on your real work, your most important undertaking. Write a page that embodies the question *What is my real work?*

Nine in the third place means that you will at first meet adversity and difficulties. Then, in time, good fortune will arrive. The nourishment of good writing projects is always there; it just takes a while for you to recognize these projects' innate value. Write a page that embodies the question *What is my greatest hurdle?*

Nine in the fourth place means that you will find misfortune. You have a writing task that is very important and that you don't feel quite up to. You must devote all your ability to that task, and you must not let yourself be distracted by frivolous people. Write a page that embodies the question *What are my strengths as a writer?*

Six in the fifth place means that if you persevere in your writing, you will eventually succeed. The important thing is to maintain an almost monomaniacal focus on your writing, and not be led astray by casual acquaintances. Write a page that embodies the question *Who am I when I write?*

Nine at the top means that excellent luck is yours. In this moving line, the cauldron has jade handles, signifying both hardiness of physical strength and softness of appearance. You are both strong and soft, and in that combination your work flourishes. Write a page that embodies the question *What should I work on next?*

## LAST WORD

This is a particularly powerful hexagram that signifies deep currents moving under your present work. Keep your mind clear and your hand steady, and your writing shall be tremendously nourished.

# 51. CHÊN

*Seek the Muse*

*Who can name you all, you accomplices of inspiration,
you who are no more than sounds or bells that cease, or
strangely new bird voices in the neglected woods, or shining
light thrown by an opening window out into the hovering
morning; or cascading water; or air; or glances.*

— RAINER MARIA RILKE

*[H]ow you come to terms with the Goddess
is no concern of mine.*

— ROBERT GRAVES

## COMMENTARY

Reverence is the keystone of this hexagram. Approaching the unknown with an open heart is one of the tasks of a writer, and it is clear that you do this task well. Keep calling out to the muses and beings who guide you as you write; they will hear your call and come to see how they can tease you or help you or send you on your way.

## PREDICTION

Once you have discovered your muse, inside or outside yourself, you will ask for her help.

## ADVISORY

Write as though your life depended on it. Write as though you had stars in your eyes. Write until the cows come home. Write, and write, and write again. You will find your way through the open land with the help of some kindly muse.

## FOR THE WRITER

Write a page of secrets about your writerly self that you would confide to your muse.

## MOVING LINES

Nine at the beginning means that you will meet your muse unexpectedly. Following the initial shock of recognition, you will find joy with your muse. Writing well under her aegis will lead to great success. Write a page of secrets that your muse would tell you, unexpectedly.

Six in the second place means you are in danger of losing your peace of mind. Danger lurks. Do not pursue the peace of mind you have lost, but wait for it to return. Write a page of secrets that your heart might tell to the rest of your body.

Six in the third place means you will be made extremely upset by an unexpected appearance of your muse. If you are spurred to action, then success will follow. Act. Write a page of secrets that you might confide to another warrior.

Nine in the fourth place means that you meet no resistance on any front. This is not necessarily good; you are not offered chances to hone your writing skills or sharpen your wit. Write a page of secrets about needing adversity to thrive. Address the page to your muse.

Six in the fifth place means danger. There are repeated shocks delivered to you by unexpected events and visits. Keep your balance by staying near the middle of the path. Call on the muse to help you cope with unruly visitors. Write a page of secrets about fear that you confide to your muse.

Six at the top means misfortune. You may lose all that you have gained by dashing ahead too quickly. Patience. You, too, will have your turn in the sun. Write a page of secrets that your muse tells you to soothe your fears and prevent your undue haste.

## LAST WORD

Muses, like many supernal creatures, are fickle and like to be wooed. They are not necessarily good or bad on their own; they simply exist to help writers and other artists compose. Be gentle with your muse. First call her out, then talk gently with her until you find out what she needs.

# 52. KÊN

## *Listen with the Inner Ear*

*I cut the cord. I said, I will do only what I can do, express
what I am — that's why I used first person,
why I wrote about myself. I decided to write from the
standpoint of my own experience, what I knew and felt.
And that was my salvation.*

— HENRY MILLER

*Moved by nameless hungers, armed with words
instead of an ax, you slip into the forest, avoiding
the trails because so many others have trampled them,
following a bird that may be leading you astray,
a wild goose instead of a honey guide.*

— SCOTT RUSSELL SANDERS

### COMMENTARY

Wisdom comes when you know how to be still and how
not to be still. You must learn when to act and when to
remain sitting. In terms of writing, this means that there
must be times when you let your work sit for a while, as
you go and collect your thoughts. Listening with the
inner ear means having the wisdom to know when to
stop writing.

## PREDICTION

You will find true peace of mind when you stop writing for a moment and start listening.

## ADVISORY

Do not stop for long. But, indeed, stop writing for a moment or two. Look up from the page and look deep inside yourself. You will find a voice that is uniquely yours — a voiceprint, as it were, speaking out to you. Listen. Then write again.

## FOR THE WRITER

Pay attention to your breath entering and leaving your body. Notice the sound of the breath leaving you. Feel the breath entering your nose. Now write the first four lines and the last four lines of a poem that meditates on what it is to breathe from deep within your body, pulling the air from deep in your seat.

## MOVING LINES

Six at the beginning means keep still. Do not write or think beyond the day's work. Listen to your heart beat. Write four lines that describe that feeling and sound. Focus, too, on whether your heart is sore or well, sad or uplifted, preoccupied by the world or well away from the world.

Six in the second place means that despite your best

intentions, you cannot stop to listen with the inner ear, to find your own voice. You are under the thrall of a stronger person than you, and that person drags you on to writing and writing — not in your own voice, not at your own tasks. This person is to be resisted. Write four or five lines in which you explore what it means to find your own voice from deep inside you.

Nine in the third place means that someone else will insist that you stay still and listen with the inner ear. But do not try to force the troubled heart to be still. Let all be organic, slow, and not forced. Write four or five lines in which you describe the shape and feel of your heart beating under stress. Now write what it is like to feel your heart beating in peace and solitude.

Six in the fourth place means that you should forget your ego altogether. Concentrate on keeping your posture straight (but not artificially so) and your breathing slow and steady. Listen, listen, and you will find your body trying to tell you some secret. Write down all that your body is saying to you.

Six in the fifth place means be silent. You may be inclined to talk a lot about your predicament, and instead it is far more important to stay still and wordless. Write nothing.

Nine at the top indicates good luck. You will listen with the inner ear, you will find your voice, and you will write with a much lighter heart. Write four or five lines in which you explore what it means to have achieved the art of listening with the inner ear.

## LAST WORD

To listen with the inner ear is no metaphor, no abstraction. It means to turn your attention away from the world and get in touch with what is truly inside. Being still is one of the best ways to listen within. Writing well consists of knowing not only what to write, but when to write. Listening with the inner ear will help you find your voice, a voice that stops and breathes as much as it chatters.

# 53. CHIEN

## *Gradual Progress*

*Generally, I write everything many times over. All my thoughts are second thoughts. And I correct each page a great deal, or rewrite it several times as I go along.*

— ALDOUS HUXLEY

*Every change of scene requires new expositions, descriptions, explanations.*

— MILAN KUNDERA

## COMMENTARY

Write very slowly today, making gradual progress. Haste will lead to mistakes. If you proceed slowly, you will have more certainty about what to write, what to change, what to erase. Further, your decisions will be better. Some perseverance is necessary so that you don't give up at this snail's pace. But if you write slowly and persevere in that course, you will be successful in your writing and revisions. An inner calm may also prevail.

## PREDICTION

You will write and rewrite this work many times, but eventually you will get it to where you want it to be. Then you will share it with other audiences.

## ADVISORY

Be careful not to forget the central impulse of your writing: to say something real in honest, authentic terms. You will be tempted to write quickly, without due consideration, and your work will suffer if you do so. Instead, take it slowly. Look back frequently at what you have already written, and make revisions with care. Look ahead to what you will write with great care, as well.

## FOR THE WRITER

Write a series of eight haiku (see Glossary, p. 279) that detail in slow, methodical terms what it is like to walk through eight different rooms — either actual rooms, as in your own house or a building near where you live, or imaginary rooms.

## MOVING LINES

Six at the beginning means that you are young in your writing process and thus should proceed very slowly. You are like a young man setting out on a journey without a mentor or a friend. Write a series of eight haiku that detail a trip, with each haiku focusing on a single leg of the journey.

Six in the second place means that you will have

good luck, which you will share with others. You are generous in spirit and in practical matters, but still caution is urged. Write a series of eight haiku in which you describe a wild goose, or any other kind of bird, looking for food in the woods.

Nine in the third place means bad luck. Do not plunge rashly into your writing or the work will suffer. Write a series of eight haiku in which a person rushes and therefore suffers.

Six in the fourth place means that you will find a way to proceed if you are clever enough. You may be surrounded by dangerous events, but if you are slow and thoughtful, you and your work will prosper. Write a series of eight haiku in which you explore what it means to be in trouble.

Nine in the fifth place indicates good luck. You will sometimes feel isolated as you write, and you may come under criticism from a friend. Nevertheless, you and your writing will prevail. Write a series of eight haiku about being betrayed by someone close to you.

Nine at the top indicates good luck. You have learned to proceed slowly in your writing, and the universe is unfolding as it should. Write a series of eight haiku about making gradual progress in any enterprise.

## LAST WORD

Gradual progress can be difficult if one is hasty or impetuous by nature. Nevertheless, at this time it is important for you to slow down and write at a snail's pace. Do not mind those who are dashing off before you. Write, and write slowly, and success will be yours.

# 54. Kᴜᴇɪ Mᴇɪ
## *Gradual Improvement*

*It was a long time before I had made a language
to my liking.*

— W. B. YEATS

*Writing is hard labor, shot through with intervals of joy.
If there were no pleasure in the sinewy turns of a sentence,
the bubbling up of an idea, the finding of a path
through the maze, who would keep going?*

— SCOTT RUSSELL SANDERS

### COMMENTARY

While hexagram 53 indicates gradual progress, this one indicates gradual improvement, which is different in that the latter denotes an upward motion toward the good. Under this hexagram, your writing will slowly get better and better, both in your process of composing and in the quality of the work.

### PREDICTION

Write patiently, and you will strike gold.

## ADVISORY

Continue to concentrate on improving yourself — your character, your ethics, your capacity for intimate relationships. And continue to write with an eye toward improving your writing. As you progress, remember to practice compassion toward your work, in your friendships and other relationships, and toward yourself. Compassion is the keystone of human life in general. Develop and practice compassion, and everything in your life will gradually improve.

## FOR THE WRITER

In your journal, write down everything you know about writing — truths both exciting and difficult. After you've jotted down five to twenty truths, stop and read them over. What do you know now about writing that you didn't know six months ago? Write down these truths as well.

## MOVING LINES

Nine at the beginning indicates good luck. You shall gain the privileges of being a successful writer without unnecessary fanfare. Remember to be modest in the face of much good that will befall you. Write down five or more truths about what it means to be a successful writer.

Nine in the second place means some disappointment before improvement. Persevere, however, and you will gain some ground. Write down five or more truths about the difficulties of becoming a successful writer.

Six in the third place implies no particular judgment. Write, progress in your writing, and you are ensured of improvement. Write five or more truths you believe about writing.

Nine in the fourth place means there will be some obstruction before your writing improves. You will wait longer than is expected. Write five or more truths about common stumbling blocks for writers.

Six in the fifth place means you will have to take second place to another writer for a while. However, as you persevere, your writing will gradually get better. Write five or more truths about humility and the writer.

Six at the top means there will be trouble. Do not just go through the motions of being a writer, but take the activity very seriously. Then you will improve. Write five or more truths about how to be a good liar.

## LAST WORD

Improvement comes through long practice and commitment to becoming a good writer. Persevere, be compassionate with yourself, and your writing will only get better.

# 55. FÊNG

*Abundance*

*Poetry, after all, milks the unconscious.*
*The unconscious is there to feed it little images,*
*little symbols, the answers, the insights...*

— ANNE SEXTON

*Thrust your hand deep into life, and whatever you bring*
*up in it, that is you, that is your subject.*

— NADINE GORDIMER

## COMMENTARY

Great success, even temporary great success, is very hard to achieve. In the case of this hexagram, it is as though it is noon with the sun at its highest heat. While all things pass, for now you are extremely successful as a writer. Enjoy your time in the sun.

## PREDICTION

You will be bold and take risks as a writer, and success — albeit temporary — will soon be in your hands.

## ADVISORY

Do not listen to the naysayers or other detractors. Practice clarity in both the generation and revision of your words. Know your abilities and demonstrate them with impunity.

## FOR THE WRITER

Imagine that you have consumed a cake that ensures your longevity. You won't live forever, but you will live for hundreds of years. What will you see around you when you are about 100 years old? Write it down, in all the richness of detail you can muster.

## MOVING LINES

Nine at the beginning means that extraordinary success will be yours for about ten days. It is a time of abundance and clarity, and you can make few mistakes right now. Write down what it means to be a successful writer.

Six in the second place means that you are lucky. You find a truth that no one else can see and hold to it tightly until everyone else sees it, too. Write down what that truth might be.

Nine in the third place means there is misfortune ahead. One of your closest allies, perhaps a writing partner, can no longer protect you. Write down what shape that misfortune might take.

Nine in the fourth place means you are lucky. You

will have much energy as you proceed with your writing, and with that energy comes much cleverness. Write down all the ways in which a writer might be clever — today and in the future.

Six in the fifth place signifies good luck. Your friends will help you with your writing. Write a fiction or nonfiction piece about what it's like to have such generous friends.

Six at the top means bad luck for as long as three months. In the abundance that characterizes your life, do not take any part of it for granted. Write down all that you think is important about your writing as it is right now.


## LAST WORD

Abundance is yours. Whether an abundance of riches or poverty is not guaranteed. However, for ten days it is likely that you will be among the most sought-after writers in the area. Success is yours, if even just for a brief while. Enjoy it.

# 56. LÜ

*Free Writing*

*[W]riting at least is a silent meditation even though you're going a hundred miles an hour.*

— JACK KEROUAC

*[N]ot everybody likes to read in order. And some do not like to write in order either.*

— MILORAD PAVIC

## COMMENTARY

Free writing is a way for the writer to get in touch with his or her own demons and delights. By writing quickly, without editing or considering readings and consequences, the writer is able to get a transparent view of his or her own mind at work. The technique of free writing is very successful in the short term. In the long term, however, more formal prose styles must be preferred.

## PREDICTION

You will travel to unexpected places in your writing through the practice of free writing. Be open to what your free writing reveals to you.

## ADVISORY

To free write is to visit strange lands and to have strange ideas; it is designed to keep the channel open between the writer and his or her mind. Pay attention to the words that come. Listen to their meanings, both articulated and hidden.

## FOR THE WRITER

Take your pen and paper and clear your mind. Choose your subject before you begin writing. Then, writing absolutely as quickly as you can, write all the feelings, sensations, memories, and questions that come to mind about the first time you did something. Sometimes writing in the present tense helps a writer remember more fully.

## MOVING LINES

Six at the beginning means that bad luck will attend you if you free write without paying attention to what's really important. Focusing your energy on trivial concerns in your writing guarantees disappointment, and maybe even disaster. Write a page or two as fast as you can about what truly matters to you, whatever that may be. Do not go back and edit or rewrite anything. *What is the most important aspect of your life?*

Six in the second place means that you will have better luck with your writing if you approach it steadily, as a daily job. Stay in touch with your inner truth and being, and all will be well. Write a page or two as fast as you can about what it means to be a traveler — however you interpret that. *Where would you like to go?*

Nine in the third place means danger. As you let go of the conventional forms of writing and try free writing instead, there is some risk that you will not remember how to return to the conventional. Patch together both the conventional and the experimental in your writing. Write a page or two as fast as you can in which you answer the question *What does it mean to be a writer in the twenty-first century?*

Nine in the fourth place means that you feel like an outsider. As you travel, in your mind and in the world, you will feel the need to stay on guard, to be ready to defend yourself against the unexpected. Write a page or two as fast as you can, addressing the question *Who are you when you write?*

Six in the fifth place means that your writing will be a real gift to someone else. Your job is simply to do the work of writing. Write a page or two as fast as you can that addresses the question *How did your life lead here, to this exact instant, in this particular place?*

Nine at the top means bad luck. It is as if all that you know and love has been lost to a fire. Proceed with caution, and write only those words that will help solve the problems brought by an anonymous person. Do not despair. Write a page or two as fast as you can about what it means to wander endlessly because one's home has burned down. What is the reality of having no home? Write in the voice of an imaginary middle-aged person.

## LAST WORD

As you free write, think about the ways in which your own mind is fluent and flexible. Then pay attention to how you might write a first draft using free writing. Think about the question *What is the equivalent of free writing in the mind?* Use free writing to make transparent some of the workings of your own mind.

# 57. Sun

*Edit Lightly*

*[A]lthough there are poems even today that I don't
find satisfactory once I have finished them, most of the
corrections I make are pretty minor. I like the idea
of being as close to the original thought or voice
as possible and not to falsify it by editing.*

— JOHN ASHBERY

*There's need of elaboration, of clarification, but I don't
know that a comprehensive revision is in order.*

— EZRA POUND

## COMMENTARY

Clear judgment and a piercing, settled mind reveal that
the task ahead is small. Proceeding in a way that is both
gentle and direct is called for. Recognize that light editing or small footsteps are all that is needed now.

## PREDICTION

If you exert even just a little effort, you will achieve great
results.

## ADVISORY

Be wary of people with big plans. Here you just need the lightest touch, a sensitive hand turned to tinkering with sounds and sentences. Beware the boor; beware of behaving boorishly in your revisions.

## FOR THE WRITER

Take three or four pages of something you have already written, and read it aloud with a highlighter in your hand. Highlight every word that seems to you imprecise or weak. Go back and change those words, then read the passage aloud again.

## MOVING LINES

Six at the beginning means that if you are too gentle, you will be indecisive. Instead, hold firm to the course you have picked, revising lightly, paying little heed to those who would claim that more extreme measures are necessary. Take a draft of something you are working on, and highlight all the verbs. Then, double-check each one to ensure that it is precise and accurate. Revise those that are not.

Nine in the second place means good fortune. People are hiding from you in the dark, making suggestions about your work that ultimately are not good ones. Instead of listening, you must pull these people into the light and reveal their carping for what it is. Take a draft of something you are working on and highlight all the sentences that are lax or loose or vague. Then go back and revise each one of those sentences.

Nine in the third place means humiliation. Too much thinking can lead to indecisiveness or immobility. This moving line indicates that risk. Take what you are working on and highlight every section of it that you have a hunch needs to be changed. Revise all the sections you have highlighted.

Six in the fourth place means success is assured if you behave properly. Do not be saddled by indecision; combine energy and modesty to prosper. Take what you are working on and let a small story about the ordinary emerge.

Nine in the fifth place means good fortune. You must pay attention to the experience you already have and revise according to that knowledge. Persevere, and you shall be fine. Take the draft you are currently working on and let your instincts guide you to what needs revising.

Nine at the top means bad fortune. You do not have the strength or outlook that will allow you to combat injury or to avoid those who would bring such to you. Take the draft you have already written and imagine reading it aloud in the sharp, hard light of sun and a clear sky. Revise those portions that sound funny in the sun.

### LAST WORD

It is very important that you be judicious and gentle in your revising now. There will be people influencing you and suggesting more extensive revision; they are wrong. Maintain contact with a handful of writers you trust, and let the work itself adjust and speak to whomever needs to hear it. Being true to the urges and heart that attend deep writing is one way to break apart from the rest of the field.

# 58. Tui

*Celebrate Your Work*

*The goal of living is not to consider work work,*
*but to consider it your life and your play.*

— GARY SNYDER

*A strong woman artist who is not afraid of herself,*
*her sexuality, passion, symbols, language, who is fearless,*
*willing to take any and all risks, often produces*
*work that is staggeringly beautiful...*

— LAURA FARABOUGH

## COMMENTARY

This hexagram signals joy, pleasure, and play. The joy rests in your strength and is evidence of how solidly grounded you are. This joy also resides in your heart. In both places, it feels gentle and contented. Be kind in your dealings with others, because you are rare and lucky.

## PREDICTION

Your writing will go extremely well.

## ADVISORY

Be careful not to dissolve into too extreme an enjoyment of life and work. You want to experience true joy — the mix of pleasure and pain that lets you know that you are really of this world. If you let yourself fly into mirth and merriment, your writing will grow too thin, superficial, stale. Feel a solid joy instead, one grounded in firmness and strength.

## FOR THE WRITER

Write a page or two in which you describe the most exotic party you can imagine, with an extraordinary guest list and setting and outstanding food and drink. Describe yourself enjoying the party, but maintaining common rules of civility and calm. You might remember the black party described in the opening pages of Huysman's *Against Nature:* the walks were strewn with charcoal, the fountain filled with ink, the dinner served on a black cloth. The meal consisted of black foods, including turtle soup and Russian black bread.

## MOVING LINES

Nine at the beginning indicates good luck. Your writing will prosper and you will feel glad. Write two or more pages in which you describe a marvelous celebration of your work, with you in the background, contented and gentle.

Nine in the second place indicates good luck. You will be tempted to copy facile, superficial writers — to go for the quick buck rather than write the deeper work of which you are capable. Don't do it. Write two or more pages in which you describe a handful of people at the center of a party talking about what brings meaning to their lives.

Six in the third place means bad luck. If you are not very careful, you will lose yourself in the idle pleasures of the rich or the lazy. Write two or more pages in which someone tempts you into base pleasures, and you resist the invitation.

Nine in the fourth place means that you will be weighing base pleasures against more virtuous acts. If you choose virtue and value over these other pleasures, your joy will be grounded. In two or more pages, reflect on the value of base acts.

Nine in the fifth place means danger. It is necessary that you protect yourself from harm. Write two or more pages in which you reflect on what could harm your writing in your daily life — and brainstorm ways to overcome that harm.

Six at the top means you may be seduced by base elements. Vanity pulls you there. Write two or more pages about the seductiveness of the glitzy and shallow parts of your world that you try to ignore. Then explain why you ignore them.

## LAST WORD

Be joyous. Let your heart sing and your contentment be grounded in simplicity and gentleness. Do not be tempted by false joy, the fleeting excitement associated with base joy. Connect yourself only to that contentment that arises from good writing and good friends.

# 59. Huan

*Gather Up the Pieces*

*When you're beginning, you think you're after scope
or direction. You're really after a believable speaking voice,
a voice that will collect feeling, the way lint collects
on certain fabrics.*

— ARCHIBALD MACLEISH

*Art is not a power, it is only a consolation.*

— THOMAS MANN

## COMMENTARY

As you write, be careful to pull together all the pieces.
You may be tempted to let the wind disperse your
words, to subscribe to the picture this hexagram represents: wind moving over water, whipping up froth and
storm. Turn your attention away from storm and toward
an easy wind. Write slowly and with genuine attention.
Gather the pieces together.

## PREDICTION

Today you will discard parts of your writing and gather up the rest into an impressive, newly arranged whole.

## ADVISORY

It is easy to get set in a particular pattern of action and thinking. Instead, let everything flow organically. Rather than hardening into winter's ice, be like water in the spring — running and rushing wherever whim takes it.

## FOR THE WRITER

Put all the pieces of your writing in the order you think you want to use. Note that order. Then try shuffling the pages or cutting-and-pasting large sections into an order you never foresaw. Try the opening scene as the very end of the story or poem. Lift out the middle of the text and split it in two; put one part at the start of the whole work and the other as the ending. Play. Treat your manuscript like water running in the spring, its path evolving as it goes along. There is no right answer, nor are there any wrong ones.

## MOVING LINES

Six at the beginning indicates good luck. Arrange your work in a particular order today, while you have the momentum and strength to do so. Write a sestina (see Glossary, p. 281) that talks about how to order a poem.

Nine in the second line means you must try to go

around the obstructions that are right in front of you. Search for your inner strength, take a deep breath, and then proceed. Write a short poem in which you explore what these obstructions are and how to get around them when you are trying to put your work in a particular order.

Six in the third place means to give up the ego. Demands on you from outside your work are so intense that you must give up the ego and let fate or the wind order your work for you. Write a short poem in which the five or six lines can be put in any order.

Six in the fourth place means fantastically good luck. Put aside old relationships and seek a new relationship with your own work. Success may seem far ahead, but it is really right in your hands. Write a short poem that describes a grand celebration.

Nine in the fifth place means you will have a unique idea that makes your whole work fall into place. Your work needs a central point, a fulcrum against which all the words balance. Write a short poem that explores what the central point of your work may be.

Nine at the top means that you must avoid danger. You do not avoid danger for yourself alone, but for your work too. Write a short poem in which you describe the risks that face you.

## LAST WORD

Disintegration of one's work is not a bad thing. It is an opportunity to gather parts together in a new way. Have the right mental attitude, be at peace inside, then let a natural excitement take over as you order your work in a new way.

# 60. Chieh

## *Face Your Limitations*

*The problem was, I had tried to be something I wasn't.
Then the most amazing thing happened once
I gave that all up: I found my voice.*

— PAT BARKER

*Poetry has always been a beggar.*

— ROBERT FROST

## COMMENTARY

This kind of limitation is actually practical. It is an effective curtailing of too grand an idea. It suggests a certain economy of motion, thinking, creating. By setting one's own limits, one is operating like the sea that finds its own shore and doesn't flood over it. Success follows.

## PREDICTION

If you know your own limits, your work will be successful.

## ADVISORY

"Write in due measure" is the guiding principle here. Setting limits on yourself — how you use your time, what you write, how often you write — is valuable. Setting limits on others is not the right path. Take your work and proceed as though you are a lake, not the ocean.

## FOR THE WRITER

Remember something (or someone) you loved very much and lost. Describe where you might have lost this thing or person, where you might find it today (and in what condition), and how that loss makes you feel. Write all this down in the form of a narrative poem (see Glossary, p. 280).

## MOVING LINES

Nine at the beginning means that you must know where to begin and where to stop. Be discreet in how you use your words. Write a flash fiction (see Glossary, p. 278) in which you explore the speech of an ordinary person who has lost the ability to talk about the disappearance of his wife.

Nine in the second place means bad luck if you do not seize the opportunity at hand. There are limits all around you, but there will be one time for action. Seize that moment. Write a short essay in which you explore what it means to wait.

Six in the third place means you have no real limitations, only seeming ones. Beware of focusing on carnal pleasures alone, because they will distract you from your far more important work. Write a narrative poem in which you describe a woman's efforts to blame someone else for missing an important opportunity.

Six in the fourth place indicates good luck. The limitation you face here is only a natural one — the limitation of pages, lines, time. Write a short poem that stops in mid stride, like Robert Graves's poem that ends with a comma ("upon a gander's wing,").

Nine in the fifth place indicates good luck. By facing your limitations — and the real limitations of your writing — you will succeed. Write a short story in which a valiant athlete makes it to the finish line in first place. Have a little suspense in the story.

Six at the top means that trying too hard leads to bad luck — and trying too little leads to bad luck. Try a plan of austerity in your writing and your life that is not too extreme. Be steady in your plan, and results will follow. Write a short story in which a woman struggles to find that middle way in her own life.

## LAST WORD

This hexagram advises facing the limitations surrounding your work, but also suggests looking at the limitations in your life. To be limited in opportunity is natural. In most cases, it is not worth fighting against these limitations because they are as fixed and natural as the tides of the ocean. However, if the nature of the limitation is harmful, then by all means try to walk through it unharmed or go around it.

# 61. Chung Fu

*Be Authentic in What You Write*

*I believe that it is almost solely from involuntary memories that the artist ought to take the central substance of his work. First of all, precisely because they are involuntary, because they form themselves, attracted by the resemblance of an identical moment, they alone have the stamp of authenticity.*

— MARCEL PROUST

*... it is the very one who wants to write down his dream who is obliged to be extremely wide awake.*

— PAUL VALÉRY

## COMMENTARY

You have a truth that is yours alone. The invisible manifests itself in your writing. Find your own voice, be authentic, let your inner truth guide the work, and you will be fine. The path of genuine speech and authentic memory is the one you must take.

## PREDICTION

You will find your stride very soon. When you do, your work will proceed naturally and with real strength. Goodness reaches your own heart, too.

## ADVISORY

Recognize the link between inner and outer lives; your interior world is represented in oblique ways in what you write. Therefore it is necessary that you scrape old paint off your palette so that your inner self is clean and clear and as powerful as the wind that stirs a lake. Do not cease in seeking the authentic in yourself, and your work will only prosper. Cut through the false.

## FOR THE WRITER

Draw a quick sketch of your body and face. If all your secrets were revealed to others around you, how would that portrait change? How would people see you? What features would you gain — horns, large ears, a huge heart, tiny hands, a body like a centaur's? Let your imagination go wild. Change your portrait. Then write about the effects of revealing your deepest self to the people around you.

## MOVING LINES

Nine at the beginning indicates good luck. Work hard on establishing inner strength and authenticity; this is the most important act. Be sharp as a knife as you pare away the false, the phony, the nice. Do not rely on others to reveal who you really are. This is work you must do alone. Write a flash fiction (see Glossary, p. 278) in which a woman turns into some other being.

Nine in the second place means there will be joy. Your words will have an effect on people thousands of miles away. Write a flash fiction (see Glossary, p. 278) in which a man turns into a white crane.

Six in the third place means you will find a friend. This friend will help you balance the moods that attend your efforts to be authentic. Draw two pictures — one of you feeling well and the other of you feeling very sad — and then write about the change that occurs between the two portraits.

Six in the fourth place means that your heart goes astray. You have trouble writing what is true. Write a page or two that center you again — that talk about how you feel right now.

Nine in the fifth place means you find the truth inside yourself. This truth allows you to write with full authenticity, in a voice and style that is entirely your own. Write a page in which you list everything that is true about you. Draw a picture of the inner you.

Nine at the top means misfortune. You can write and write today, but nothing comes out true. Take a rest, then write two pages that explore why it might be that the authentic voice will not come today. (It may be impossible to find your voice as long as you are preoccupied by trying to hide some truth about your own life.)

## LAST WORD

It is a cliché, but one of the most important aspects of your work is to be authentic — to write in your own voice about your own subject, and in your own way and style. Such advice is easy to give, but to undertake writing in real ways is often painful and difficult. Nevertheless, this place of authenticity is usually the source of the best writing you do. Persevere in this course.

# 62. HSIAO KUO

*Play with Your Punctuation*

*As a poem comes to me, in the process of saying
and writing it, the lines themselves establish a basic
measure, even a sort of musical or rhythmic phrase
for the whole poem. I let it settle down for quite a
while and do a lot of fine-tuning as part of the revision.*

— GARY SNYDER

*[P]unctuating can change the whole meaning,
and my life is full of little dots and dashes.*

— ANNE SEXTON

## COMMENTARY

Punctuation is a small aspect of writing. But getting it right sets the tone and sharpens the content. It can help in establishing character. Punctuation is nothing exceptional, except as a cue to oral delivery. You must control that aspect of your writing, too.

## PREDICTION

You will be modest about your own efforts in general, but you will work very hard to get the sound of your lines exactly right.

## ADVISORY

If you are conscientious in how you punctuate your work, success is assured. Play with the sounds of your lines and ensure that you use commas, semicolons, dashes, and periods to indicate exactly how you wish your work to be read. Be quietly modest in your efforts, but know that these small efforts contribute to the overall effect in absolutely essential ways.

## FOR THE WRITER

Start with a page of existing writing. Now play with the punctuation. Start by using commas to express the emotion and pacing (see Glossary, p. 280) of the piece. Don't worry about "the rules" for this exercise. Remember that, in some ways, "She slowly reached for the knife and then threw it as hard as she could," is not as effective as, "She, reached, for, the, knife, and, then, threw it as hard as she could." Commas are designed to indicate a breath or a pause. Periods indicate a longer pause. Dashes are often used in informal writing or dialogue. Choose all the places in your work where you seek to have your reader pause. Put a dash, a comma, a semicolon, or a period in these places.

## MOVING LINES

Six at the beginning means bad luck if you fly through punctuating this piece. You must concentrate, because this task is in all truth very serious. Take a small section of your work and completely redo the punctuation to make it sadder. Then do it again to make the tone angry. Finally, redo the punctuation in this section so that it expresses exactly the tone and mood you hope to convey.

Six in the second place means your work is more serious than you see. It is important to get the punctuation exactly right, to ensure that the lines are delivered in a somber tone when appropriate. Take your own writing and change a page of it so that it conveys a tone of seriousness where you wish it to. Use punctuation, especially marks that signal long pauses, to express that seriousness.

Nine in the third place means bad luck. There is danger ahead unless you are extremely cautious. Consider each change with care. Take a small section of your existing work and pay attention to those punctuation marks you are taking for granted, that you find insignificant. Those are the ones that must be changed.

Nine in the fourth place means to change nothing at all. Start a new piece, something short, in which you describe the rhythms of clouds scudding across a clearing sky.

Six in the fifth place means that all is unclear. It is murky and you are foggy when you think of how to change the punctuation in your work. Nevertheless, if you take a stab at it, it is sure to come out better.

Rewrite the first page of something from a magazine, paying particular attention to the rhythms that can be emphasized by changing the punctuation.

Six at the top means bad luck. You will miss the punctuation that needs changing and skim right by it. It is necessary that you slow down and even halt at times, so you can see what obviously must be changed. Take a section of your work-in-progress and circle every punctuation mark you have. Then read your work aloud exactly as it is written. Go back to the punctuation marks and try changing every other one. Then leave some of those new marks, revert to some of the old ones, and try reading it aloud again. Keep repeating this exercise until the whole piece is revised and sounds exactly as you wish.

## LAST WORD

Pay attention to the small. What seems insignificant is, in fact, of utmost importance. If you don't get the punctuation right, the delivery of the writing will seem false or unclear. Punctuation is especially necessary in poetry and in fiction's dialogue. Feel free to use punctuation in unconventional ways. Be cautious but exacting as you pay attention to ordering your work in this fashion.

# 63. CHI CHI

## *When You Are Done*

*Any true work of art has got to give you the feeling of
reconciliation — what the Greeks would call catharsis,
the purification of your mind and imagination — through
an ending that is endurable because it is right and true.*

— KATHERINE ANNE PORTER

*Closure. The art of closing. One of the most important
things in all forms of art is the closure. This goes for life
too:... the life which is lived well in all its dimensions
from beginning to end will have a close which
follows beautifully and naturally.*

— WILLIAM EVERSON

## COMMENTARY

Although you have arrived at a point where the work
might be called done, it is very important that you are
cautious in celebrating what you have finished. Yes,
there is order to your piece. Yes, there is a certain satis-
faction about what you have written. Nevertheless, this
hexagram reminds you that it is essential not to take its
worth for granted. Disorder could follow if you do.

## PREDICTION

You will be prematurely pleased with the completion of some writing.

## ADVISORY

Do not think that you are completely done with this draft. Everything may seem in place for the moment, but when you try to tinker with it one last time, there is the risk that all will fall apart. Take it slowly, read your work aloud, and listen for places that might need change. Do not throw away your old draft when you make those changes. Ask a friend who is a writer whether the changes improve your work or not. Keep working until they do.

## FOR THE WRITER

Find a place in your existing work that you think is completely done. Crack it open. Try to rearrange the parts, change the punctuation, or play with character and line. Shift some parts around one last time before you settle on the shape of the final draft. As you scrutinize your writing one last time, celebrate its near-completion even as you move its parts around.

## MOVING LINES

Nine at the beginning means that you do not see the necessity of making changes. You have already put on the brakes and think you are done. Look at a draft you think of as nearly final, and rip it apart. Change everything — point of view, character, names, punctuation, verbs, everything. See if it improves; if it does not, reassemble the work with a few other, more gentle changes.

Six in the second place means it will be at least a week before you finally complete your draft. In the meantime, hide your work from the curious. Take your draft and privately revise it again. You need only to be patient as you revise these pages one last time. Let no one else read it until you are done.

Nine in the third place cautions that you must not show your work to those who are inferior readers. Take your finished work and ask an experienced friend to read it. While you wait, write something fresh and revise it. If you can't find a topic, write about the first time you climbed a tree.

Six in the fourth place means you must be careful all day long. There is a hidden problem with your draft, and you must discover it and work cautiously on it. Take your draft and put it away for much of the day. Then retrieve it and work slowly on each sentence, improving each one according to syntax — how the words fit together — and content. Be gentle with yourself as you write, and your writing will show a gentle hand at work. Find out what is hidden and start your work there.

Nine in the fifth place means you will not be happy with small revisions. It is necessary that you follow the lead of great revisers, such as Katherine Anne Porter or William Everson (quoted in the epigraphs for this hexagram). Take a finished draft and revise it one more time. Be thorough and sweeping in your revisions at first, just to loosen you up. Then go back through and see which revisions you really want to keep. Do not be chary, small, or miserly in your first revisions. Break open the work.

Six at the top means genuine danger if your work remains the same. Do not retreat to what you have already written, but try new things. Take a passage in what you have already written and read it aloud. Study it. And then, when you revise it (as you must, according to this moving line), avoid vanity and admiration of your great work. Simply move forward, revising more than you think necessary, never looking back.

## LAST WORD

It is easy to be premature in saying that you are done, or done except for some small tweaking or tinkering. According to this hexagram, you only think you are done. In fact, there is revision still remaining, revision that must spring from clear vision and a peaceful mind. Be attentive to other ways of speaking and being, and then connect those to the work you are doing on the page. As always, the visible and the invisible are indivisibly connected.

# 64. Wei Chi

*Before You Are Done*

*[In the immediate present] there is no perfection,
no consummation, nothing finished. The strands are
all flying, quivering, intermingling into the web,
the waters are shaking the moon.*

— D. H. LAWRENCE

*... the struggle seems to be to uncover things by language,
to find out what you mean and feel by the sheer effort
of writing it down.*

— ELIZABETH HARDWICK

## COMMENTARY

This hexagram counsels caution as well as celebration that you are nearing the end. Its season is spring, when the ice breaks and the fruit trees are close to fully flowering. Be careful, but proceed.

## PREDICTION

You are closer to finishing the work than you realize.

## ADVISORY

To rush is a mistake right now. Take it slowly. You do not want to be the person who skates rapidly across the spring ice only to feel it crack under him. Be clear but cautious. It is easy to have order turn into disorder if an attentive eye is not kept on the work.

## FOR THE WRITER

Take a deep breath. Then plunge into your writing afresh, top to bottom. Imagine that you are reading it from the perspective of a diver, or someone else who doesn't know much about your topic. Where do you need to develop your ideas? Expand in those places.

## MOVING LINES

Six at the beginning means humiliation. You try to revise too fast, the ice creaks underfoot, and you fall into the water. Take out your work and look it over. It is necessary to proceed much more slowly than you intended as you revise. Hold back from rushing. Ask yourself where it is best to begin, start there, and make yourself take an extra long time with each section you revise. Slow down.

Nine in the second place means if you go slowly enough, you will have good luck. You know how to stop and tinker with a sentence. Take out your work-in-progress and go at the pace you know you should. If you put on the brakes where instinct dictates that you should, and concentrate your revision efforts there, your work can only improve.

Six in the third place means that if you attack your work, misfortune will follow. It is important to have an attitude of gentleness toward your work and charity toward yourself. If you work too hard and viciously on self or work, disaster follows. Take out your work-in-progress and get yourself in the right frame of mind — perhaps through making a cup of tea, taking a brief rest, or simply watching yourself breathe. Then proceed with genuine care to revise your work.

Nine in the fourth place means struggle. You must be thorough and resolute as you revise. Take out your work-in-progress and wrestle with the words. Trust your instincts and be strong as you revise somewhat ruthlessly. Do not fall into easy acceptance of your own work.

Six in the fifth place means you will have good luck if you are steady and sure in your revisions. Take out your work-in-progress and be quite clear in your efforts at ruthless revision. Out of the ruins of your manuscript will grow genuine beauty and value if you make the necessary corrections.

Nine at the top means that all will be well if a certain propriety is observed. Celebrate your work and the fact that you are near the end, but do not let your exuberance overshadow the work yet to be done. Take out your work-in-progress and read it to yourself. Then write a letter to yourself in which you offer advice on how to revise it.

## LAST WORD

The last hexagram of the I Ching suggests beginning as well as ending. Having the last hexagram symbolize "nearing completion" indicates that we must go back to the first hexagram to understand the full cycle of events and lives. Note how we are part of this web of meaning and distraction. If you are strong and clear in every step of the writing process, maintaining an awareness of your authentic self, the I Ching will offer some direction. Always be aware of how the future arises from this present. Always be aware of how much our actions matter, no matter how unimportant we think ourselves or our work to be.

# MORE PRACTICE
# FOR THE WRITER

## WHAT NOW?

As a writer, you might decide that you need to develop your composing process in more depth. You might recognize that practice is the key to becoming a better writer. Or you might decide that the exercises and predictions offered by individual hexagrams aren't of the flavor you had hoped for. Whatever your motivation, this part of the book will offer an expanded set of exercises designed to help you flex your writing muscles a little more. Here you'll get more practice in what makes good writing tick.

We all hold to the wishful thinking that the best writers don't revise, they write purely from inspiration. Some people believe in a sort of Platonic ideal, an imaginary, perfect text (one writer calls it "a ghost text") that hangs over the text you're composing right now. Everyone half-believes that if only you could capture the words and form of that ghost text, then you would write brilliantly.

My college students often hold to this particular

school of thought. They believe in the Beat Generation's credo, "First thought, best thought." What they don't know, however, is that even the very best writers among the Beat poets and storytellers and playwrights and memoirists used to revise their work repeatedly. The well-known Beat poet Allen Ginsberg even went so far as to have other writers work on his poems — which he then published under his own name! Almost all of the time, writers of any real ability or capacity rely on knowing their craft as they write and revise endlessly, and as they lean on friends who also know the writer's craft. While all writers hope to experience that lightning flash of inspiration that reveals what to write, very few actually get that lucky.

The truth is that it's rare and lucky to be struck by inspiration, to write with depth and resonance the very first time. Inspiration of that sort is about as likely as the birth of a pure-white buffalo. It's not that it doesn't happen, it's just that it so rarely does. While pure inspiration does happen once in a while, most of us have to write, and rewrite, and rewrite again.

## *The Value of Extra Practice*

The value of extra practice, such as that offered in this part of the book, is that you get better at the writing and rewriting. I thought I knew how to write after having completed all the papers and theses required for my two master's degrees. But it wasn't until I wrote my PhD dissertation, a bear of an exercise that turned out to be more than 200 pages long, that I understood what it means to write something long, clear, and with heart. Those pages were more scholarly than the essays and reviews I've written for, say, *Parabola* or *Tricycle*, but the process is roughly the same: write, rewrite, and rewrite again.

## A True Story of Writing a Book

Here's the truth of how I wrote my first book. I'm a writer who procrastinates and then "binge writes" close to the deadline. (To be honest, that's what I'm doing right now!) So, even though I'd been thinking about writing my first book (an academic one about computers and storytelling) for more than a year, it wasn't until November of my sabbatical year that I really tackled the project. Here's what I did: I would get up in the morning, eat some breakfast and get some coffee, and then, still in my pajamas, I would sit down at our kitchen table and write all day. I'd shower before dinner. And while I'd break for lunch and dinner, usually I would write after dinner, too. Dinner sometimes was just take-out food from local Indian or Chinese restaurants. I worked seven days a week. (I've read that the novelist Beryl Bainbridge also belongs to the write-in-your-nightgown, pull-down-the-shades, and eat-take-out-food school of writing.)

Once I'd finished my first draft and revised it, I couldn't keep track of all the changes I was making. And I definitely needed to revise the second draft, and then revise it again. So I bought a notebook and cut-and-taped sections of the book onto its pages. After several more revisions, I had assembled the entire book — about 300 pages of manuscript — across the pages of two or three notebooks. Then I went back to my computer for the fourth or fifth draft, and I performed the revisions and the cut-and-paste exercises that I had done on the pages of my notebooks.

I finished the book sometime in February.

## *The Writing Process for Professional Authors*

Conversations with other authors confirm that the writing process is always individual, even idiosyncratic, and usually a little messy. For every writer I know, writing is a process of rethinking and rewriting, page by page, chapter by chapter. Experienced writers know that what you're thinking of as the *last* five pages of a story or essay might become the first five pages. Writers like Isabel Allende know that some of the best endings come in dreams, and she revises accordingly. Ernest Hemingway is rumored to have rewritten the ending of *A Farewell to Arms* forty-two times. And the short-story writer Judy Doenges talks about most of her writing as really being rewriting. Her stories typically go through at least a dozen drafts.

And once you know that revising is the norm for professional writers, a sort of relief can come over you. You suddenly realize that you're not alone in not getting it right the first time. If you're lucky enough to belong to a writers' group and talk to its members, you'll see this truism borne out by their experience, too. Write, rewrite, and then rewrite some more.

## The Five Stages of the Writing Process

Some writers see the writing process as falling into five major stages. In my experience, these stages are too neat a description of the messy, recursive process that writing is. They leave out the daydreams and walks and conversations that are part of writing, too. Nevertheless, thinking of your writing in terms of these five stages can help you organize what you want or need to do next in your work-in-progress.

These five stages are commonly construed as brainstorming; planning; generating a first draft; revising the draft; and polishing. These stages roughly correspond with a chronological description of writing.

Brainstorming is an electrical metaphor for the way ideas emerge: unbidden, previously unseen, mysterious. Planning is the stage at which writers take the material generated by the brainstorm and sort it out. What part will you work on first? Where does the ending come? Who will tell the story? Generating a first draft is the toughest work. You sit down and actually execute the plan you've worked out. In addition, however, you have to stay open to the unexpected turn the story might take, the character who might appear out of nowhere, the shift in the weather, the good guy who turns bad. You write the poem or story from start to end. Then you revise that draft, paying attention to where you need more detail (or less), considering the point of view and the voice, rearranging the material, and imagining how readers might respond to particular scenes or stanzas. Finally, only at the very end do you turn your attention to the polishing (copyediting and proofreading) that all writers have to do.

What follows is a list of alternative exercises, each connected to a hexagram. You might decide that the hexagram exercises already provided just don't interest you. Or, again, you might decide that you just want more practice in writing. I've also indicated which exercises might fit best with the stage of writing you want to practice, irrespective of the hexagram it appears under. (Tying together the stage of the writing process with individual hexagrams yields loose associations at best. Nevertheless, it's fun to play at each stage, as you feel you need to.)

Finally, I invite you to play as much as you want with these exercises, picking out those that appeal, jettisoning those that leave you cold, and altering them to suit your purpose. Writing is actually an enjoyable act sometimes, and I hope you find some of the following exercises just plain fun.

## HEXAGRAM EXERCISES FOR EACH STAGE OF THE WRITING PROCESS

1.  BRAINSTORMING
    Hexagrams: 4, 10, 13, 16, 23, 26, 27, 51, 55, 56, 61.

2.  PLANNING
    Hexagrams: 7, 8, 11, 14, 15, 19, 20, 37, 44, 45, 47, 60.

3.  GENERATING
    Hexagrams: 1, 5, 6, 17, 25, 29, 35, 39, 43, 52, 54.

4. REVISING

   Hexagrams: 2, 3, 12, 18, 21, 28, 31, 32, 36, 38, 41, 42, 48, 53, 59, 64.

5. POLISHING

   Hexagrams: 9, 22, 24, 30, 33, 34, 40, 46, 49, 50, 57, 58, 62, 63.

## ALTERNATIVE EXERCISES
## FOR EACH HEXAGRAM

### 1. Begin Again

There is a swing set inside your head, two small children playing on it. They start to talk about their lives ahead. What do they say? Where are they headed? You have the power to look into their future. How right are they? What will really become of them? Write a two-scene skit, the first scene in the present, the second scene twenty years later.

### 2. Grounded Writing

Write a short scene about a sanitation worker removing the rubble from an abandoned lot in Manhattan. He finds an object he wishes he hadn't and turns it in to the police.

### 3. Address Difficulties

Write down all the negative experiences you have had with your writing. Then imagine each one dissolving in the rain.

## 4. Embracing Darkness

Write a poem about trying to get to the moon.

## 5. Pause

Take a household object — something like a honey jar — and describe its height, weight, substance, color, and shape in exquisite detail. Have a friend draw the object from your description and see how accurate you were.

## 6. Writing Dangerously

Think of someone real who you love, work with, or know well. Write in stream-of-consciousness (see Glossary, p. 282) style about the nightmare they had last night, then write about what would happen if that nightmare came true.

## 7. Be Strong

Write a limerick about a bodybuilder who likes to wear silk dresses.

## 8. Seek Harmony in the Whole

An unexpected visitor gives you a gift: twine, glue, a button, a yard of magenta cloth, a single tube of yellow acrylic paint, a nightgown, a recording of an opera, and a raven. Write a poem in which you describe the process of making something with these materials.

### 9. Pay Attention to the Details

Imagine you have been asked to join a club that requires you to wear a certain uniform. Describe the uniform in close detail. Then describe the same uniform after it has come back from an accident at the dry cleaner's.

### 10. Find the Writer's Path

Close your eyes and imagine an animal who is going to show you the writer's path. Listen to what he or she is saying and then write down every word.

### 11. Write in Peace and Quiet

Take off your shoes and socks and place one bare foot in the center of a blank page. Trace the foot. (Then put your shoes and socks back on, if you wish.) Inside the outline of the foot, write a poem about walking. On the outside of the outline of your foot, in a pen or pencil of a different color, write a series of short sentences about the pleasures of travel.

### 12. Obstacles Are Opportunities

Write a two-party dialogue, in which one party is an obstacle you are facing and the other party is you. Have the obstacle explain to you why it persists in the form it does, and reason with it.

### 13. Be Aware of the Creative Voices Inside You

Write the lyrics to a rhyming song that expresses loss and the wish to find the right road.

### 14. Acknowledge a Great Vision That You Already Possess

Write a paragraph in which you explain to a close friend what you are trying to do in the work-in-progress. Then write another paragraph in which you explain how you are going to realize the vision you have for this work. Finally, write a last paragraph that sketches a rough timeline for the work you shall complete.

### 15. Develop a Humble Attitude

Using the device of interior monologue (See Glossary, p. 279), describe a creature of humility, for example, a mouse, a silent man, the last member of a tribe.

### 16. Enthusiasm

Look at your feet. Write down everything you think about your own shoes. Then write the first draft of a long poem that talks about taking a joyous walk wearing those shoes.

### 17. Follow the Writer's Path

Take a ride on some mode of public transportation — a subway, bus, or trolley — and write a short stanza or three sentences about what you see at every stop. If you can't actually take the bus, imagine it all.

## *18. Revise Your Work*

Find a passage in your existing work that needs revision. Take a highlighter and highlight every word, phrase, or sentence you wish to keep in that passage. Then, working just with those highlighted sections, rewrite the passage.

## *19. Overseeing the True Way*

Write a short sketch about a man whose memory operates in a way different from most of ours.

## *20. Observe*

Find a plant, a blade of grass, a shrub, a bonsai, or a small tree. Study it closely in every way that is available to you. See it, smell it, taste it. Look at it upside-down. Feel its textures, observe its color and shape, its size in relation to others like it. Does it look like a letter of the alphabet? Does it look like the shape of anything familiar? Write a close description of that plant, starting at the bottom and working your way up. Ascribe a magical power to the plant. Use it to cast a spell or to heal someone.

## *21. Persevere in Your Work*

Start by listing three chronic problems in your abilities to work. Brainstorm three ways to overcome each problem. Be both practical *and* respectful of your creative work as you brainstorm.

## 22. *Put in the Delicate Touches*

Circle all the verbs in the piece that you are working on. Examine each one to be sure that it has some punch, lucidity, specificity. Remember that verbs are the words that carry the freight in any one passage.

## 23. *Strip Away Illusion*

Draw five animals that stand for the delusions you labor under as a writer — delusions good or bad. (They might run the gamut between complete lack of self-confidence and delusions of grandeur.) Then, next to each animal, write a description of the delusion it stands for. Meditate a little on the qualities of these animals, then relegate them to the margins of your mind. Draw one last animal that suggests the true way.

## 24. *Return to the Work*

Circle ten words in today's newspaper. Then choose the first name of one person mentioned in the newspaper and the last name of someone else mentioned there. Combine the two names. Write five sentences about the person whose name you have invented, each sentence using two of the ten words you have circled. Then rewrite your five sentences so that they take place in one of the following settings: (a) the front lines; (b) a bickering office community; (c) a New York City subway; or (d) a dirty hotel.

### 25. Write Spontaneously

Write a manifesto about the importance of flutes and pennywhistles in building a democratic society.

### 26. Hold Firm to Art's Exquisite Path

Write a poem about a heavenly beard that grows shorter every day.

### 27. Nourish the Life of a Writer

Look at your own face in the mirror and slowly draw it on a piece of paper. Then sit down with your picture and write a short character sketch (see Glossary, p. 277) about the person you see there. Who is it? What does he or she do for a living? What is he or she thinking about?

### 28. Crisis in Writing

Write a flash fiction (see Glossary, p. 278) that takes place in one twenty-four-hour period and involves a fierce argument about a pet.

### 29. Danger in Writing

Imagine your writing as something that hurts, or that is capable of inflicting pain. Where is the pain located? Write about that pain.

### 30. Enlightenment

What is your very first memory? Write down that memory.

### *31. Find a Writing Partner*

Drink a beverage. Describe the sensation as it enters your mouth, touches your tongue, slides down the back of your throat. Try to use verbs more than adjectives or adverbs in your description. Now read it to a willing partner and see if that person can guess what beverage it was. Drink it again, then write again, until you get the description of it exactly right.

### *32. Endurance*

Write a poem or story about a girl who wakes up from a coma. She reunites with her family in very slow gestures and words.

### *33. Turn Away from Those Who Would Weaken Your Writing Practice*

Put on your slippers or a pair of your most comfortable shoes. Remove three distracting objects from the immediate setting of your writing. Write about the effects of their removal.

### *34. The Power of Great Style*

Describe the inside of your mouth to somebody blind.

### *35. Progress*

Draw your own hand, then draw it again. Describe your thumb in such detail that someone else could draw it without seeing it.

### 36. Overcome Writing Difficulties

Imagine your writer's vision as a kitchen utensil. What utensil is it? Why? Write a poem or story in which you talk about the kitchen from the point of view of that utensil.

### 37. Write What You Know

Look at the day's local newspaper. Using the actual first sentence from an article you find interesting, write the rest of the story in a new way.

### 38. Revision

Try writing your draft to your best friend or your worst enemy.

### 39. Move Ahead Despite Obstructions

Pick a first name randomly from the phone book, then pick a last name randomly from the same book. Write this person's interior monologue (see Glossary, p. 279), concentrating on his or her many failures at work.

### 40. Work on the Ending

Imagine that you are persevering against all odds in an activity such as climbing a mountain, overcoming cancer, swimming in a triathlon, or singing the lead in an opera. Describe a photograph that shows you just at the moment when you come to the very climax of your activity.

## 41. Shorten Your Writing

In five sentences, describe a con man's pair of hands as he holds a handful of cards in a poker game in Las Vegas. In four sentences, describe just one of his hands holding the cards. In three sentences, describe just one finger as it taps a card the con man is considering whether to play. In two sentences, describe just one fingernail of that hand tapping a card. In one sentence, describe the air between a con man's fingers and his cards.

## 42. Expand Your Text

Choose a particular paragraph or passage in your own writing. Then put on a soft piece of music. As you listen, develop the section of your work-in-progress that you have chosen.

## 43. Writer's Block Overcome

Imagine that you are walking alone at night down a dark and empty street. The trees are whispering, storm clouds gather. It's very late. On your right, out of a narrow doorway, steps the most frightening person you can imagine. Who is it? What does he or she say? How do you respond? Write the scene.

## 44. Beware of Misfortune

Take colored pencils or crayons and draw the first thing that occurs to you when you think of happiness. Now do the same thing for enthusiasm. Write a poem about either picture.

## 45. Form a Writing Group

Draw a picture of the most unenthusiastic person you can imagine. Put the drawing aside. Now draw a picture of the most enthusiastic person you have ever seen. Put the two drawings side by side, and write a dialogue between these two people.

## 46. Achievement Is Near

Become a muse who discovers a piece of paper with writing on it. What does that piece of paper say? What does the muse do with it when she or he is finished reading it? How does the muse incorporate the piece of paper into her own imaginative life? Write about the piece of paper from the point of view of the muse.

## 47. Take a Short Rest

Write a dramatic monologue (see Glossary, p. 277) from the point of view of a woman deep asleep and dreaming.

## 48. Face Your Writing Demons

Write a flash fiction (see Glossary, p. 278) about a hiker being tormented by a stinging insect.

## 49. Work on Transitions in Your Writing

You are a hippie living in a commune in southern Oregon. Describe your living quarters. Now describe them after the police have upended the place looking for drugs.

## 50. *Auspicious Refinement*

Ignore all writing until you've taken a bath or put some part of your body in water; at the very least, wash your hands. Then summon your muse by writing a short poem to her. Tell her you wish to refine your writing process. What does she say in response?

## 51. *Seek the Muse*

Warm up today by writing two pages in which you invoke your own muse. First describe the characteristics of the muse. What does its voice sound like? What is it wearing? After you have described everything you can see or hear about your muse, take a deep breath and close your eyes. Listen to what your muse is saying. After thirty seconds or so, open your eyes and begin writing everything it is saying to you. At the end of the exercise, thank it. Ask it to return.

## 52. *Listen with the Inner Ear*

Close your eyes and visualize your heart. Now hear your heart's voice. Write down everything it tells you.

## 53. *Gradual Progress*

Light a match and watch it as it burns. Write a haiku (see Glossary, p. 279) that captures the spirit of that moment. Now write a haiku about that same match gradually growing cold and useless.

## 54. Gradual Improvement

Imagine a doctor who lives inside you. He wanders through your body and mind, fixing what he can. What does he look like? What does she say? Imagine your own doctor and watch him or her for a while. Then write it all down.

## 55. Abundance

Make up a character who is in some kind of financial trouble. Give him or her a check for three times as much as is needed to settle all debts. What does the character do? Write about this.

## 56. Free Writing

Find a comfortable spot and sit there for five minutes, eyes closed, watching your breath. Count your breaths in sets of ten. Try not to let your attention wander beyond the edges of your breath. At the end of five minutes, open your eyes and start writing whatever comes to your mind. Write fast and furious. Don't stop to edit or think. Just write and write and write. If you can't think of anything to write, simply keep writing some sentence like, "nothing is coming to mind right now; nothing is coming to mind," until you think of something else to say. Then take a red or green pen and circle three places where you like what you have written. Free write (see Glossary, p. 278) about each of those places on a separate page.

## 57. Edit Lightly

Choose a passage on which to work. Look at the sentences in that passage. Are they sufficiently varied in length? Try adding a very short sentence (or sentence fragment) on occasion. Write at least one tremendously long sentence by either combining existing sentences with commas and semicolons and dashes, or adding a new sentence altogether. Place a long sentence and a very short sentence side by side. Read the work aloud and keep playing with the length of sentences and the pacing until it sounds right.

## 58. Celebrate Your Work

Using five-sense imagery (see Glossary, p. 278), describe your dream vacation spot in great detail. Write about how it would nourish you. After writing at least two pages about this pleasure spot, close your eyes and feel yourself go there.

## 59. Gather Up the Pieces

You are a high-school music teacher with wanderlust. Write yourself into some trouble.

## 60. Face Your Limitations

If you wear glasses, take them off. If you don't wear glasses, find a pair to put on. Think about the problems of vision, and how being visually impaired might make one feel. Write ten sentences, short or long, describing eyeglasses that bestow special powers on whoever wears them.

## 61. Be Authentic in What You Write

Take four ordinary household objects and put them on the table in front of you. After you have chosen your objects, imagine that each one is a facet of you as a writer. Write down how each one represents your innermost self.

## 62. Play with Your Punctuation

Outline a story that will bring its readers extravagant joy. The story should involve a bear, a circus, an umbrella, and a unicycle. Use punctuation in unexpected ways.

## 63. When You Are Done

Write down fifty things you can do with a paper clip. Do five of them and write a humorous vignette (see Glossary, p. 283) about one of them.

## 64. Before You Are Done

Go outside with pen and paper and find the nearest road. Write down everything you see and hear on that road for at least ten minutes. Then go back inside and write the first page of an essay, poem, or story set on or near that road.

# FOXES AND DEER OF
# THE IMAGINATION

When I went through the process of getting tenure at the University of Puget Sound, a different fox crossed my path each step of the way. Literally. It was eerie. I saw a total of three red foxes, each on the day of an important decision in my tenure case — a fact I wrote about in my last book, *Digital Fictions: Storytelling in a Material World* (Greenwood, 2000). I've sighted them twice since at important junctures in my life. I've gotten used to the idea that foxes visit at some of the most important crossroads in my life. Foxes and writing are now closely aligned for me. They both develop under cover of darkness, scavenge materials from the oddest sources, and have a sly, sideways approach to the dangerous art of living fully, of composing themselves against the daylight.

But a new animal presence helped me in the composition of this book.

One fall evening last year, after a tough meeting, I left campus and found myself driving around the foothills. It had been raining all day. For no reason, I turned down lots of closed roads — gravel roads, fire roads, dirt roads. I guess I just wanted to explore. Eventually, I turned down a closed road that stopped just before a washed-out bridge. I pulled over to the side of the road, turned off the engine, and rolled down the window.

It was near dusk.

It was still so wet. I looked out over sodden pastures. Dylan Thomas knew vistas like these: "Oh as I was young and easy in the mercy of my means/Time held me green and dying/Though I sang in my chains like the sea." Time held me green and dying on that road.

Then the sun broke through and lit the pastures around me in a supernatural green.

As I sat gazing out at a field brilliant, fecund, and wet, to the south the sun lit up the back of a herd of mule deer angling toward a wire fence that marked one pasture's border.

One by one, the deer leapt gracefully over the wire fence, each clearing it by a good three feet. Soon six, then ten, deer were eating the grass soft with rain, each deer spotlighted in the pasture by a late-evening sun, my imagination grazing with them. The day's leaden weather split open and released all that sunlight onto the backs of those deer. The dusk's glimmer united field and animal, and as I idly gazed, the idea for this book approached: I could write a version of the I Ching for writers. The topic of this book arrived somehow through my watching the deer leap, then graze, then amble, alive in imagination's light, their sleek shapes stark against the chance green-and-gold field.

All this is true.

Working with the I Ching for over twenty years has taught me the importance of chance connections in making sense of the world.

Somehow the mule deer are involved in my writing this book, but I can't say exactly how. All I can in good faith say is that they were there when I thought of what I should write about. On some level I listened to the deer, and on some level they spoke to me. The deer offered a lesson in how important it is to sometimes follow instinct, feeling, or gut response, as we encounter the unexpected and unpredictable genius of our world — and our imagination thriving within its limits.

## THE I CHING AND THE IMAGINATION

The I Ching helps writers develop their imagination. But where do imaginative ideas come from? Of course, nobody really knows. Literature is full of accounts of people who go to bed at night with a problem and wake up in the morning with the answer. Story endings come in dreams. John Fowles had only an image of a girl standing by the water in heavy fog when he started writing *The French Lieutenant's Woman*. Watson and Crick supposedly got a glimmer of the DNA helix when one of them went slalom skiing. Some musical composers claim that the music is channeled through them, and they just write it down. One writer I know had no idea how events around her kept turning up in her fiction. One time a woman driving in the opposite direction lost control of her car, sailed across the lawn of an apartment complex, and hit a tree. Within a week, a car accident scene had entered a draft of my friend's novel — but she had no idea about where the scene had come from.

Legend has it that William Faulkner chased after his characters with a pencil in his hand and wrote down everything they said. Jorge Luis Borges liked to write prompted by antique prints and sepia photographs. Other writers have similar rituals of mind and eye to help them in their work. In each case, however, I would hazard that writers are simply using different heuristics to turn imagination's spotlight onto the stage of memory and anticipation, regret and hope, that are the creative writer's primary materials.

The truth is we can't answer our own question. Imagination sometimes just surfaces, a familiar being that started out unknown, unpredictable, and dreamlike. It is a ghostly substance that is unghosted by our minds. We don't really know how imagination works, but we can see what it does. It is a process, and we are primarily privy only to the product: stories, poems, books, and other works of art. Throwing the I Ching is also a process; it is imagination tugging at our sleeves. But once it is thrown, process turns into product, and a hexagram is the visible result.

## PUTTING IN THE DELICATE TOUCHES

As I finish writing this book, it occurs to me to try an experiment first attempted by psychologist Carl Jung. In his famous introduction to the Wilhelm and Baynes translation of *The I Ching or Book of Changes,* Jung explains that just before he wrote his introduction, he threw the coins to see what the book itself felt about its current situation. Jung was uneasy about endorsing a Chinese divination instrument; he himself was no sinologue, and some respected scholars saw the I Ching as superstitious "magic spells." He threw the I Ching to allay his worries and satisfy his curiosity. He sought, he said, "...to enter a dialogue with an ancient book that purports to be animated." The I Ching's response did not disappoint Jung.

Jung's answer was hexagram 50, Ting, translated as "The Cauldron." He read the hexagram as the voice of the book talking to him, and what the book said was, indeed, encouraging. Jung interpreted this image as a sort of soup kettle containing cooked food, food that stood for the spiritual nourishment offered by the I Ching. In his analysis of the two moving lines in his hexagram, he saw further evidence that the I Ching understood itself as rich and nourishing. However, the I Ching's influence was small because it was largely disregarded and unrecognized by contemporary readers: "the fat of the pheasant is not eaten."

In my experiment, I likewise personified the I Ching. Very close to finishing this book, I asked the I Ching a similar question to Jung's: "What does my book feel about its present situation?" The response I got was hexagram 22, "Adornment" or "Grace" in standard translations, and "Put in the Delicate Touches" in my own adaptation. No moving lines.

I read "Put in the Delicate Touches" as meaning,

first literally, that I had to do one last light revision of each section of the book. I was pleased that the Advisory said that this hexagram was "best selected toward the end of the writing process." Second, though, more metaphorically, I saw the book suggesting to me that I remember the delicate moments in life, including, yes, again, the crepuscular light of the imagination. The soft shades of dawn and twilight are the most delicate and mysterious moments of our lives. The moment of the deer in the dusk was a visit guided by chance and imagination, a moment real but also almost supernatural in its easy collaborations between the dusk and the deer, their shapes soft and improbable against the wet field. "Put in the Delicate Touches" is a mandate to make sure that the imagination has its delicate voices — mysterious in origin but mellifluous in expression — heard, too.

Both interpretations of this hexagram are relevant to the composition of this book.

## FINAL WORDS OF ADVICE

I do believe that all ideas come from interpretation of existing facts, experiences, or intense memories. Even the best conjectural science fiction has its feet planted firmly on the ground; it reaches into contemporary science and simply maps out some potential trajectories. All imaginative writing is rooted in real experience, and it is in real experience that we find our best ideas.

However, our imagination stirs those experiences and gives us new and creative readings of that which we know already.

This all means that our imagination is only as rich as our storehouse of images and impressions. Maybe that is why the poet Madeleine DeFrees advised her graduate students to keep feeding the imagination — that that was one of the most important activities one could do as a writer. The I Ching can shake us up with the accuracy of its forecasts, but it really is simply a moving ground against which we can figure our own stories.

If you have worked with these I Ching hexagrams for a while, doing some of the writing games, revising your work according to suggestions, and reading through the extra writing games, you may have picked up a new facility of writing. Probably you'll know more about how to brainstorm, plan, generate a draft, recast material, and polish your work. But more important, I hope you will have a new sense of how to play with words, invent scenes and sounds and settings and stanzas, and recognize your own innate creativity. You will have learned how to work with your own imagination.

So my last messages of this book are that, yes, writing is hard work; yes, there is no substitute for the work of writing and rewriting, sometimes many times; and, yes, conversation and shared critiques are often useful parts of the game. But there is another yes, too: There can still be a touch of mystery to writing, moments not foreseen, ideas that just arrive. You may catch the deer in their field just before the sun goes down. You may know yourself better by letting your interpretations of the I Ching just go wild. Find the connections, listen with the inner ear to the secrets of the heart.

Writing is a matter of hearing snippets of an unexpected song inside your head or heart, of finding a diamond in the coal bin. It is crucial to give your imagination latitude, to always stay open to imagination's rare genius. If you are to write, it is an absolute necessity — as well as an inimitable luxury — to listen for imagination's subtle music, this magic that arrives unbidden.

# GLOSSARY

## *Definitions of Literary Terms*

**CADENCE:** From Latin, "a falling." The rising and falling of the voice in speech, a pattern that often gives free verse its rhythms. Also the rising or falling of speech at the end of a sentence, a pattern designed to emphasize the musicality of language.

**CHARACTER SKETCH:** A quickly written "picture" that describes the overall features, quirks, and looks of someone real or imagined. The "picture" should provide in words a convincing likeness of a real person or made-up character.

**DRAMATIC MONOLOGUE:** A long speech given by a character in a play, story, or poem. Always given in the voice of a particular character, some dramatic monologues are written just for the audience or reader (rather than for the other characters in the drama).

**ENJAMBMENT:** The way a line in a poem continues into the next line without a break. Different from the so-called "closed" line because these lines flow (or "run on") from idea to idea without the customary punctuation at

the end of each line. Often used in free verse or blank
verse (the latter being defined as verse that follows a
strict metrical pattern but doesn't rhyme).

FIVE-SENSE IMAGERY: The use of all five senses (taste,
smell, touch, sight, and sound) to describe a place,
person, or thing. Joseph Conrad frequently used this
technique in his novels.

FLASH FICTION: A very short story, with the usual elements of plot, climax, pacing, and style, but taking
only 250–750 words to tell it.

FREE VERSE (in French, *vers libre): A poetic form that
does not conform to any traditional rules of rhyme
or rhythm. Instead, free verse (first used by Walt
Whitman and the Modernists) relies on the rhythms
of speech, enjambment, and a more natural line
length and line break. Also known as "unmetrical
verse," this is the primary form of poetry written in
the United States today.

FREE WRITING: A process of writing that requires the
writer to move her pen or pencil across a sheet of
paper as fast as she can. The writer must never stop
writing; when stymied, it's okay to write the same
sentence over and over. Something like "I don't know
what to write" or "I can't stop writing" or "I'm going
to write more soon" usually works to propel the writer
back to other topics.

GENRE: Related to the word "generic," this refers to a
type of writing. In fiction, it is often used in a faintly
pejorative way to designate conventional types, such

as westerns, science fiction, thrillers, romances, mysteries, or horror stories.

**HAIKU:** A Japanese poetic form, often described as being about nature and consisting of three lines, with five syllables in the first and third lines and seven in the second. But a haiku can, in fact, be a seventeen-syllable poem arranged differently, or be any very short poem, often about the seasons. The main point of a haiku, as developed by Basho, is to offer an impression or image of the moment, often a moment outdoors. Haiku is sometimes related to the immediacy in the practice of Zen Buddhism.

**IAMBIC PENTAMETER:** A rhythm of line often said to resemble the beating of a human heart. Alternating soft and strong stresses, the writer composes lines of ten syllables each, with every two syllables made up of a "soft-strong" stress.

> When asked to be a bouncing ball I say
> to you, "I think, my friend, it's not at all
> the thing I had in mind..."
>
> — SARAH JANE SLOANE

**INTERIOR MONOLOGUE:** A conversation with the self that takes place inside a person's head but is overheard by the reader. Not likely in drama, it is a technique that works well in fiction and poetry when the writer wishes to reveal the inner workings of character and motivation without telling the other characters. Different from stream of consciousness in their coherence and lucidity, interior monologues probably don't accurately represent the associative, fleeting, and disjunctive patterns of how we actually think. Different from a dramatic monologue in that it takes place only inside a character's head.

**MAGIC REALISM:** Coined by Alejo Carpentier in 1949, the term "magic realism" describes a particular combination of everyday events and the supernatural, or magical, in fiction. Originally, magic realism dipped into local legends or religious beliefs for its supernatural elements, but today magic realism describes almost any combination of ordinary events and the supernatural, especially in stories written by Latin American authors.

**METER:** The rhythm, number of syllables, stresses, or length of a line, usually of poetry. Playing with all or some of these metrical measurements usually adds to the pleasure of reading.

**NARRATIVE POEM:** A poem in any form (e.g., free verse, blank verse, rhyming) that tells a story. Usually the story has a clear beginning, middle, and end, with a narrative arc rising to a climax toward the ending, but not always. A narrative poem can also tell just part of a story. Distinguished from a lyric, which usually describes a moment, or perhaps a series of moments, without any narrative component.

**PACING:** The rhythm of a poem or story, or the rate at which either one moves. Writers play with the form of sentences and lines, as well as punctuation, to create different paces for their readers. Fragments, run-on sentences, or lines punctuated with a series of semi-colons are all ways to play with the pacing of a story, a poem, or even a speech in a play.

**PROSE POEM:** A poem in the form of a paragraph or several paragraphs, or simply in a block style (justified prose written without paragraph indentations). In other words, prose poems do not have a ragged right edge, nor do they follow the dictates of formalist poetry (or even free verse). A prose poem is distinguished from prose by its economy of words, distillation of image, or use of poetic flourishes that are more typically found in conventional poems. A genre that is actually hard to define, a prose poem is really any prose that has poetic elements and that its writer says is a prose poem.

**PROTAGONIST:** The primary character in a story or narrative poem, who performs the primary action of the piece. To be opposed by the "antagonist," who is usually the person, being, force, or thing that holds up the protagonist from accomplishing what he or she has set out to do.

**SESTINA:** A specific poetic form that requires a deft hand, with words repeating in a particular order. The sestina has seven stanzas (lines of a poem that work together in a group, separated by white space above and below), and six end-words are repeated in a different order through each of them. The first stanza establishes the initial six end-words. Then each of the stanzas plays with those end-words in the following fashion (each letter stands for a line ending in a particular word):

Stanza 1: A B C D E F
Stanza 2: F A E B D C
Stanza 3: C F D A B E
Stanza 4: E C B F A D
Stanza 5: D E A C F B
Stanza 6: B D F E C A
Stanza 7: All six end-words, two per line, three lines total.

"Sestina," by Elizabeth Bishop, is an excellent example of this form.

**STREAM-OF-CONSCIOUSNESS:** Language in poetry, fiction, or plays that echoes the chaotic, inchoate words and images typical of thought. Often seemingly random and associative, stream-of-consciousness writing is creative work's best guess as to how the mind works.

**URBAN LEGEND:** An unsubstantiated story or legend, typically situated in a city, with apocryphal details about some unlikely, often horrific, event that happened there. These stories are passed by word of mouth, and often ascribed to someone twice removed from the teller. Entertaining and almost always untrue, urban legends are a staple of any sustained gossip or contemporary storytelling about the city.

VIGNETTE: A short scene or sketch designed to illuminate larger themes or happenings within fiction or
poetry. Typically not directly related to the relentless
engine of plot, a vignette is a simple, usually detailed,
scene that fleshes out the story. The term can also
refer to the graphic design that historically appeared
at the beginning or end of a storybook.

# KEY FOR IDENTIFYING
## THE HEXAGRAMS

| TRIGRAMS<br>UPPER ▶<br>LOWER ◀ | CH'IEN ☰ | CHÊN ☳ | K'AN ☵ | KÊN ☶ | K'UN ☷ | SUN ☴ | LI ☲ | TUI ☱ |
|---|---|---|---|---|---|---|---|---|
| CH'IEN ☰ | I | 34 | 5 | 26 | 11 | 9 | 14 | 43 |
| CHÊN ☳ | 25 | 51 | 3 | 27 | 24 | 42 | 21 | 17 |
| K'AN ☵ | 6 | 40 | 29 | 4 | 7 | 59 | 64 | 47 |
| KÊN ☶ | 33 | 62 | 39 | 52 | 15 | 53 | 56 | 31 |
| K'UN ☷ | 12 | 16 | 8 | 23 | 2 | 20 | 35 | 45 |
| SUN ☴ | 44 | 32 | 48 | 18 | 46 | 57 | 50 | 28 |
| LI ☲ | 13 | 55 | 63 | 22 | 36 | 37 | 30 | 49 |
| TUI ☱ | 10 | 54 | 60 | 41 | 19 | 61 | 38 | 58 |

# ABOUT THE AUTHOR

Photo by Craig Hollow

Sarah Jane Sloane is a working writer and associate professor of English at Colorado State University. She lectures frequently on topics ranging from how to get started as a writer to the element of chance in writing. Her poetry has been published in numerous journals and her creative nonfiction and book reviews have appeared in *Tricycle* and *Parabola*.

She is the author of *Digital Fictions* (Greenwood, 2000), a consideration of how computers are changing literacy and the literary practices of reading and writing fiction. She has studied at Oxford and the University of Edinburgh and holds a BA from Middlebury College, an MFA from University of Massachusetts at Amherst, an MA from Carnegie Mellon University, and a PhD from Ohio State University. She lives in Fort Collins, Colorado, where she teaches, paints, and throws the I Ching.

New World Library is dedicated to
publishing books and audio products
that inspire and challenge us to improve
the quality of our lives and our world.

Our products are available
in bookstores everywhere.
For our catalog, please contact:

New World Library
14 Pamaron Way
Novato, California 94949

Phone: (415) 884-2100 or (800) 972-6657
Catalog requests: Ext. 50
Orders: Ext. 52
Fax: (415) 884-2199

E-mail: escort@newworldlibrary.com
Website: www.newworldlibrary.com